Tidings of Comfort and Joy

A Collection of Holiday and Heart
Reflections to Last Throughout the Year

CHERYL BERGER

WestBow
PRESS
A DIVISION OF THOMAS NELSON

Scripture taken from the New King James Version. Copyright 1979, 1980, 1982, 1985 by Thomas Nelson, Inc. Used by permission. All rights reserved.

Cover artwork and interior pen & ink illustrations by Stacy Jordon. Used by permission.

ISBN: 978-1-4908-0573-3 (sc)
ISBN:978-1-4908-0575-7 (hc)
ISBN: 978-1-4908-0574-0 (e)

Library of Congress Control Number: 2013915120

WestBow Press books may be ordered through booksellers or by contacting:

WestBow Press
A Division of Thomas Nelson
1663 Liberty Drive
Bloomington, IN 47403
www.westbowpress.com
1-(866) 928-1240

Printed in the United States of America.

WestBow Press rev. date: 10/03/2013

Dedicated to the flickering stars that have graced the
skies of my life, and to Jesus, the One true light.

For Kim,
     Whose prayers usher in
the presence of the Prince of Peace.
May His peace continue to rule
and flow from you ♡.

                    Cheryl

TABLE OF CONTENTS

INTRODUCTION

It was 1991. The church we were attending was in the middle of rehearsals for that year's Christmas drama. I don't remember where I was coming from that afternoon, but I was running late. So I parked the minivan in the carport adjoining the babysitter's house, left the engine running and went inside to pick up our two youngest before heading to the church.

Our oldest, nine year-old Veronica, was helping the sitter's children pick up the toys scattered around the living area. Securing two year-old Nathan in his car seat, I buckled five year-old Samantha into her booster seat next to him. I was in the middle of paying the sitter when the house reverberated with a loud crash. We looked up to see the window's air conditioner unit dangling over the television where one of the babysitter's kids was sitting. It seems Samantha had unbuckled herself, climbed into the front seat, gotten behind the wheel of the minivan, put it in gear and somehow managed to drive forward, crashing into the babysitter's truck and house. Fortunately no one was hurt, there was minimal damage to the house and vehicles, and we didn't have to search for a new childcare provider. I really wish I could have been a fly on the wall at the insurance company when my husband called to file an auto accident report on our five-year old driver.

By the time we arrived at rehearsal that evening, the church hotline was buzzing about the adventures of Samantha "Andretti." That Christmas I wrote a poem regarding our family's adventures, of which the above incident was highlighted, and included it in our Christmas cards. The response was positive and I was encouraged the following year to write another. Since then, a Christmas poem or short story has been composed and included in our annual cards as my personal gift to family and friends. Twenty plus years later, I have been encouraged to compile them, as well as some of my other writings, in the collection you now hold within your hands. I have probably covered a little bit of everything except the kitchen sink . . . no, that was covered, too.

In all honesty, this compilation originally started out being a Christmas devotional of sorts. But since almost every holiday piece had a theme that could be applied to everyday life, one by one, non-seasonal pieces were added. Because I like to know the reasons or motivation behind why an author writes a certain piece or a worshipper selects a particular song to sing, each one has an introduction that gives a little insight into why it was written. Also included are correlating scriptures to be used as a reference. All written to encourage others with the hope found in Christ.

To all of those who have either been on our Christmas card list or offered words of affirmation regarding my writing, I thank you. Your encouragement has given me the confidence to continue putting pen to paper. And to Jesus, whose love stirs my heart and tongue to be the pen of a ready writer, please receive my composition concerning the King. For You, O Lord, are worthy.

It is my prayer that the messages contained in this anthology speak to your heart and bring you *Tidings of Comfort and Joy.*

~ *Cheryl Berger*

THE TREES DIVIDING our property from that of our neighbors were waving their branches, as if trying to get my attention. I was lonely. We had just relocated three thousand miles, leaving a community, a church and a people we had grown to love. I remember looking out the window from my kitchen's alcove that day, watching the leaves scattering in the wind, when a thought blew across my mind. Lay down your cares and trust God. *A New Season* was my response.

"Therefore, humble yourselves under the mighty hand of God, and He will exalt you in due time. Casting all your cares upon Him, for He cares for you.
(1 Peter 5:6-7)

A New Season

Looking out my window, I see the changing of the seasons. Foliage once green is now burgundy, copper, mahogany and gold. The rich, earthy colors make one feel warm amidst the cool winds of autumn. And as I find pleasure in the changes about me, I realize that not only do the seasons change in nature, but in our lives as well.

Looking inward, I find myself entering a like season in life. As the leaves have been falling outside, blanketing the ground in autumn splendor, the Creator has been calling to me in the wind. His voice has been rustling the foliage of my own life, calling me to cast them upon Him. *"Casting all your cares upon Him, for He cares for you."*

And as I listen, it is the words preceding that verse that pierce my heart. *"Therefore, humble yourselves under the mighty hand of God, and He will exalt you in due time."* Humble yourself. Before we can cast our cares upon Him, we must first humble ourselves, surrender our wills to Him. We must fully realize that we cannot handle life's situations in our own strength, even those our mind tells us we can. For we were not made as trees, to be weighed down with leaves, no matter how light, no matter how colorful. No, our branches are to be lifted in praise to the One who created us.

So as the cares of my life continue to wither and fade like the changing of the leaves, I pray that I will humble myself completely. Casting all of my cares upon Him so that I can stand before Him as a tree in autumn. Unhindered. In so doing, as in nature, the Creator can begin a new work in me. A new season.

Looking out the window of my heart, I see the ground around

me blanketed with the cares of my life. How free I feel as the winds of change rustle through my now bare branches. And though these said winds are cool, I am warmed, for I am filled with the presence of God's love. My fallen leaves bear witness. He really does care for me.

ALL OF US have been affected by the declining economy, some more than others. Many have experienced irritating inconveniences, while others unsettling devastation. A wise man once said *"There is a season for everything; a time for every purpose under heaven."* And just like the changing of the seasons, change comes into our lives as well, times of loss, as well as gain. So as we trust in the One whose breath blows upon the earth sifting the sands of time, we know that He also holds our lives in His hands. And He is more than able to make everything beautiful in His time.

"My soul, wait silently for God alone; for my expectation is from Him."
(Psalm 62:5)

"To everything there is a season; a time for every purpose under heaven . . . a time to break down and a time to build up."
(Ecclesiastes 3:1, 3)

"But seek first the kingdom of God and His righteousness, and all these things shall be added to you. Therefore do not worry about tomorrow, for tomorrow will worry about its own things. Sufficient for the day is its own trouble."
(Matthew 6:33-34)

TIDINGS OF COMFORT AND JOY

D arkness seeped through star-studded skies like spilled ink on white canvas. Feathery crystals frosted the ground in iridescent layers of light, while evergreen trees bend under the weight of winter's glory. Trumpeting the season, frigid winds blow across frozen lakes, whose waters sparkle like diamonds in shimmering shades of gray. Nature's offering of holiday joy.

Inside a modest duplex, a middle-aged woman sits quietly at her bay window, face turned towards illumined skies. Salty teardrops fall in time to nature's iced confetti. Flickering flames from her marble fireplace add little warmth to the chill seeping throughout her anguished soul. For the umpteenth time, she replays the somber chorus that had been this past year's running theme. What she wouldn't do to hear the joyous sounds of Christmas playing contentedly within her ravaged heart.

For the year had brought unexpected sorrows. A recessed economy had not only emptied their 401k, but had tendered a premature retirement, causing her husband's spirits to spiral into a life-altering depression. Harsh words, angry silences filled their once-happy marriage. Vows were broken, possessions divided, as their life together was split in two. Starting over, unfamiliar dressings now adorn her rented dwelling place. Faded photographs capture the joys of the past; disappointments overshadow the present, while casting doubts on a promising future. And the tears continued to flow.

Her silent evensong is broken by the sound of heavy footsteps on her icy walkway. Throwing open the front door she is embraced by her co-workers, neighbors and a handful of strangers. All with arms filled to overflowing with holiday faire. Mirroring their happy banter, melancholy turns to delight as the merry sounds of the Season sift through her heart with sprinkles of comfort and joy.

Inviting aromas whet their appetites as they position themselves around the blazing fire. Mismatched plates are filled with traditional delicacies, while a homemade cobbler cools atop her kitchen's granite countertop. Hope burns within her as she realizes though change had brought devastation, it had also brought new life. For each of those gathered around her had also experienced various levels of difficulty over the past year. Some had lost jobs, homes, loved ones, while still others had been diagnosed with unwelcome health issues. Yet each one had put aside their troubles to help ease the suffering of another. And for a moment around a roaring fire, all was calm; all was bright. For memories are made of hearts joined by adversity as well as love. Bowing their heads, she offers grace for unexpected blessings. And Heaven and nature sing.

This Christmas finds many singing the blues as holiday hearts are burdened with unforeseen pressures. Conversations are peppered with songs of simpler times. Times when recession, unemployment and foreclosures were but irregular heartbeats on this musical staff called life. But amidst these discordant notes, runs a hidden melody, one heralding peace on earth, goodwill toward men. *For to everything there is a season, a time for every purpose under heaven, a time to break down and a time to build up.* And this is a time of new beginnings. For God makes all things beautiful in His time.

Random winds may have blown through your life, scattering all that was familiar. Circumstances may have caused you to lead your life in quiet desperation, fearful of what tomorrow may bring. But take heart. For as the Creator feeds the birds of the air and clothes the lilies of the field, so He can and will do so much more for you. Valued above all of creation, you are the song of His heart. And He loves you.

Radiant beams of hope shine upon waiting hearts. Star-crossed skies glisten with quiet whispers of peace. All the while nature sings His tidings bringing comfort and joy. As should we.

O tidings of comfort and joy.

FOR SOME REASON, this next piece *Bid Me Come* is one of my mom's favorites. One she is quick to share with those whose lives rarely extend beyond the walls of hospitals and nursing homes and with those in the throes of grief. To those feeling like the waters of adversity are threatening to overwhelm you, grab hold of His lifeline of hope, walk out upon the seas of His presence and allow Him to take you safely to the other side.

"Cast your burdens on the Lord, and He shall sustain you;
He shall never permit the righteous to be moved."
(Psalm 55:22)

"When you pass through the waters, I will be with you;
and through the rivers, they shall not overflow you."
(Isaiah 43:2)

Bid Me Come

The storm clouds hovered over me
Streaks of lightning flashed my fears
As life's whirlpool pulled me downward
Drowning me in bitter tears.

Cast me, Lord, a line to cling to
I'm overwhelmed by what I see
And yet You walk upon the waters
Bidding me to come to Thee.

Bid me come across the waters
Bid me walk upon the seas
Of my troubles, cares, my burdens
Bid me come and walk with Thee.

Fear grips me in its talons
Yet your arms of grace draw near
And so I step out upon the waters
Where faith replaces fear.

And though the storm rages about me
As the waves beneath me swell
With my eyes fixed on my Captain
My heart knows all is well.

Bid me come across the waters
Bid me walk upon the seas
Of my troubles, cares, my burdens
Bid me come and walk with Thee.

A gentle peace flows deep within me
As the seas of life are calmed
Hope, a rainbow hangs above me
Safe, secure within Your arms.

Bid me come across the waters
Bid me walk upon the seas
Of my troubles, cares, my burdens
Bid me come and walk with Thee.

Bid me come, my faithful Captain
Bid me come and walk with Thee.

THE ENTRANCE OF God's word brings light because God is light. Every year, many communities kick off the Christmas Season with a grand illumination, a holiday event that draws people together for ceremony. But here's a thought. What if the annual tree lighting did more than brighten the night skies of a community, but dispelled the darkness in men's hearts as well. From that thought came *The Angel Tree*.

"Do not be afraid, for behold, I bring you good tidings of great joy which will be to all peoples. For there is born to you this day in the city of David, a Savior, who is Christ the Lord."
(Luke 2:10-11)

"Behold, I make all things new."
(Revelation 21:5)

THE ANGEL TREE

Moonlight shimmers upon crystal ice like glittering tinsel on the legendary white spruce. Its wispy green branches seemed to glisten from within under luminous lunar rays. A gentle wind tickles the air with hopeful expectation. Swirling snowflakes waltz across the skies in winter's enchanting ballet, while prickly pinecones play peek-a-boo between needle-like leaves.

It was Christmas Eve, the evening of the Annual Grand Illumination. City officials and invited guests had gathered together in the town's main square on a cold, wintry night. Warm-hearted volunteers passed out cups of steaming hot chocolate. Bundled up in sheepskin and wool, happy children clapped excitedly as strings of clear miniature lights twinkled in time to Heaven's celestial ornaments. Joining a chorus of carolers, townspeople and visitors made merry the sounds of the Season, as Heaven and nature sang.

This year's chosen evergreen with its long, willowy branches, boasted more notable gaps than pine needles; its treetop more crooked than straight. And yet illuminated, the result was spectacular for beauty was displayed in simplicity. Unique also was the ceremony itself. Though more celebrated tree lighting events whet the appetites of audiences with famed celebrities and musical artists, this community featured guests with a more local flavor. Feasting on tales and music of yesteryear, town leaders and residents regaled personal tidings of comfort and joy. Some recollections produced laughter, while others triggered tears; still each one a welcome reprieve from the frenzied holiday rush and a reminder of the true meaning of the Season. Hope. And hope can be found in the most unlikely of places.

Affected by a depressed economy, many businesses had gone under and the once-thriving community had become a mere shadow of its former glory days. Legend has it though, that watered by tears of oppression, hope grew unexplainably in the middle of Town Square that Christmas Eve. Gathering around the ceremonial tree, Christmas memories drifted like snow through the hearts and minds of all who were present and they experienced an unexpected peace. Suddenly, a dazzling light illuminated the promenade, causing many to shield their eyes from its brightness. Clad in a flowing garment of radiant white, waist fitted with a belt of gleaming bronze, an imposing figure hovered above the decorated spruce. Ebony tresses framed a strong, handsome face. Piercing dark eyes mirrored the hue of the midnight sky. And like a timpani, it's rich, baritone voice resonated through the air like thunder, silencing the awestruck crowd.

"Don't be afraid," he began. "I bring you good news affecting your entire community. For this night the bright light of hope has dispelled the darkness and your time of recession is over. The One who knows all and sees all has seen your difficulties and heard your cries. Find now relief, as His hands of blessing are open and extended toward you. Receive His free gift of benevolent grace. For from this moment on, your burdens are lifted as He makes all things new. So take heart and be at peace, for behold, the help of your Savior is suddenly upon you."

As quickly as the angelic presence had come, it vanished, its incandescence fading in the dense snowy mist. In its wake, the tree glimmered and shone with an ethereal radiance. A multi-faceted star was its crowning glory, while jewel-toned orbs dangled from snow-laden branches. Each one inscribed with an encouraging word.

To this day, no one knows exactly when and how the ornaments were embossed or how they were able to address each person's specific need. And yet, that is exactly what took place that magical evening. While gazing upon the tree, an answer relating to a particular circumstance would stare back at them like written words on a mirror. Bodies were healed and strength restored to those needing healing. Those in need of comfort were given relief as despair turned into praise. The hungry were fed, homeless given shelter and the lonely were clothed in a warm embrace. If that wasn't enough, the unemployed found employment. Those struggling were given ideas to thrive and prosper. While estranged relations were reconciled as offenses gave way to forgiveness. A community came together for a ceremony, but left with so much more. And they gave thanks for unexpected blessings.

One such instance was that of a middle-aged woman standing pensively in the Square. It was midnight; the crowds had long dispersed and yet the soft, steady glow from the tree's crystal lights beckoned her to linger. Elegantly dressed, her need was not financial. It was not material. It was not even physical. No her need was something quite different. Held captive by fear and insecurity, her life was but a smoldering ember of the flame it should have been. And her heart was filled with dark shadows. Yet as the snow continued its feathery descent, its fragile flakes mingling with her tears, her eyes were drawn to a crimson colored ornament. Instead of an imprinted word, however, its embellishment was a golden cross. And she knew what she must do. Kneeling down, the Square became a sanctuary, the angel tree an altar. Surrendering disappointment and regret, her heart was made new while the falling snow baptized her in the moonlight. All was calm; all was bright, as waves of peace flushed out her soul's bitter waters. And like the others before her, she gave thanks for the gift she was given.

Hundreds of miracles like this one were documented that night and countless others have since followed. And like the promise given by the heavenly messenger, all things were made new. Businesses, lives, hearts. For on an ordinary night, under diamond-studded skies, an unsuspecting town experienced a Christmas miracle like none other. Hope was renewed in God and in their fellow man. Its magic continues to this day. A replanted evergreen stands as a lasting reminder of an enchanting midwinter night's dream.

And dreams do come true, but life is not a fairy tale. Answers and blessings don't grow on trees. They do, however, flow freely from on high for there is an angel tree in Heaven. Not like the one illustrated above nor even those on display in department stores during the holidays. No, this one is in the form of a Savior, one who lights our way through the dark valleys of decision. Who knows our needs even before we ask. Gift wrapped in God's love and cradled in a manger, Jesus came to earth over two thousand years ago with an offer of salvation. Since then His life has been the source of hope and inspiration to a multitude of believers. For engraved upon the palms of His hands are the names of those made in His image. Those whose faces and needs are always before Him . . . yours and mine.

And He oftentimes sends various messengers relaying His goodwill toward us. They can be heard in the gentle voice resonating loving concern and in comforting words of grace. Seen in selfless hands helping us through trying times and in those that wipe away our tears. They can be felt in the heart that forgives our offenses while accepting our differences. Held in strong arms that shoulder our burdens, binding us in a tender embrace. And then there are those that bring unexpected blessings. Like the bearer of a timely check that cancels a financial debt or a random conversation that creates an opportunity. Or how about the deliverer of floral sunshine that brightens an otherwise cloudy day. Divine miracles resolving in this symphony we call life.

Discordant notes may flow through the melody of our lives causing missteps along the way. But God's plans for us are for good and not evil, to give us a future and a hope. And He longs to bless us above and beyond even our wildest dreams. All He requires is that we ask. Ask and believe. So during this time when we reflect on the past and look forward to the future, may our hearts sing a carol of blessing, as we give thanks for all we've been given.

Yawning skies awaken the dawn as the sun rises over the sleepy little town. Morning mist settles upon the ground stirring creation from its slumber with a whispery kiss. Stretching its limbs towards the sky, the celebrated spruce welcomes the new day, its evergreen boughs permeating the air with the sweet incense of pine. While tranquil blue skies fill the atmosphere as far as the east is from the west, as does the love of the Creator. He really does make all things new.

REGENERATION. SURRENDER GIVES birth to desire. And desire gives wings that we might fly. *Spread Your Wings and Fly* was written when I found myself out on a limb, wrapped up in a cocoon of God's promises.

"But those who wait on the Lord shall renew their strength; they shall mount up with wings like eagles, they shall run and not be weary, they shall walk and not faint."
(Isaiah 40:31)

"Now faith is the substance of things hoped for, the evidence of things not seen."
(Hebrews 11:1)

Spread Your Wings and Fly

Sunlight filters through billowing clouds drifting aimlessly across azure blue skies. Its radiant light brings warmth to the earth and its inhabitants.

On the ground below, a small caterpillar slowly inches its way forward. Fueled by an intense fire burning within, it is not hindered by the many obstacles blocking its way. For within its tiny frame burns a desire, a desire to fly.

In the natural, it would appear impossible for a wingless creature to soar the skies above. Yet the caterpillar does not look at the situation with its natural eyes, but with the eyes of its heart. And the fire does not wane.

Drawn to tree branches waving freely in the breeze, the thought occurs that this might be a means to the fulfillment of its desire. And so it climbs. Not looking at what is seen, but what is unseen. Looking only to the hope burning within.

Reaching the top, it discovers a world it did not even know existed. One filled with beauty and treasures beyond measure. How it longs to be a part of this new world, to soar beyond the heights upon wings of desire. Taking a deep breath, it begins its mental checklist for take-off. But then, reality sets in. Desire has not birthed wings. There can be no flight. And it collapses in frustration upon an emerald green leaf.

Tired, disheartened, with a need to hide itself from the outside world, it spins for itself a silk-like covering. Closing its eyes, it drifts off into a dreamless slumber. Hope dies and the fire is extinguished.

Yet as the weeks pass, it is strengthened. A flame of hope begins flickering softly within, as does the longing to fly. Slowly releasing itself from its cocoon, it is pleasantly surprised as newly formed wings unfold from its frame. Flapping them in excitement, it leaps with joyous abandon into the air. Instead of plummeting to the ground, however, its wings carry it across the once-forbidden skies. With the light of the sun as its guide, it flies. It soars. Hope burns anew as desire is fulfilled.

You, Child of God, are as that butterfly. Desire burns within you to fly the friendly skies of your Father's world. To soar above the rainbow of His promised blessings. But you are hindered. You have no wings. The fire of your faith has become a smoldering ember. And you are weary. Yet as did the butterfly, you must find a quiet place and enclose yourself in the cocoon of your Father's arms. Be strengthened as His love enfolds you. Find fullness of joy as you rest in His presence. And soon, you, too, will soar, rising high above your circumstances upon wings of faith.

Behold, the light of the Son filters in, dispelling dark gray clouds of hopelessness, bringing warmth to the very depths of your soul. Rejoice as His rainbow of promise majestically adorns your skies. And, arise, Child of God, arise. Cast off your binding grave clothes. And spread your wings and fly!

PASSAGES. THERE ARE times when our lives hit an iceberg and we find ourselves shipwrecked on unexpected seas of calamity and change. And though these interruptions are a surprise to us, God is not surprised. For He alone is able to set our sails aright and lead us safely to our destination. When adrift upon my own seas of change, *Ship of Dreams* came to me after watching a movie on the *RMS Titanic*.

"Fear not, for I am with you; be not dismayed, for I am your God. I will strengthen you, yes I will help you, I will uphold you with My righteous right hand."
(Isaiah 41:10)

"Fear not, for I have redeemed you; I have called you by name; you are Mine.
When you pass through the waters, I will be with you; and through the rivers, they shall not overflow you. When you walk through the fire, you shall not be burned, nor shall the flame scorch you."
(Isaiah 43:1-2)

SHIP OF DREAMS

It was a starless night when the great ship embarked upon her maiden voyage out onto the oceans deep. Within its many cabins was a menagerie of talents, treasures and people alike. Its diverse cargo of passengers came from different walks, different society levels and sported different values. Some had saved for years their meager earnings to book passage, while others took for granted the luxuries the ship afforded. Yet, all were aboard. All were looking forward to the voyage ahead. All were filled with the hope and dream of a brighter tomorrow.

As the Titanic set sail, its majestic flags waving proudly in the breeze, little did the travelers realize they were aboard an ill fated vessel; one that would never reach its destination. Their dreams were about to be dashed against an immovable block of ice, and buried in a watery grave beneath a midnight clear. Bright hopes of tomorrow swallowed up in liquid darkness.

On this leg of my life's journey, I, too, feel as though I have hit an iceberg. Jolted from the sudden impact, my voyage has come to an abrupt halt. Fear assails my senses as the lower levels of my vessel fill rapidly with raging waters. My dreams seem out of reach, sinking slowly beneath the surface, and with them, seemingly my hope.

Do you ever feel this way? Are there times in your life when you boarded what you thought to be a Ship of Dreams, only to find yourself shipwrecked? Are your hopes and dreams floating aimlessly upon the seas of life, some even plummeting into the depths below? Are your limbs becoming numb as you bob up and down in the frigid waters? Has your vision become blurred, leaving you feeling lost and without purpose?

Beloved Drifter, be not dismayed. Though cool, brisk winds of life whip mercilessly about you, and treacherous waves threaten to overturn you, there is no cause for alarm. For your Captain has not abandoned ship. He remains on board upon the watery deck. Even though the vessel seems to be sinking, He is at the helm, steering your life in the direction of His choosing. While you may be uncertain about your whereabouts or even your destination, He is not troubled. His compass is in His hands, and He stands ready to set sail upon the troubled waters of your life. For He knows the plans He has for you, plans for good and not evil, to give you a future and a hope.

Open your eyes and see. He stands before you now, casting out a lifeline to which you can cling. Grab hold and anchor your faith in His words of hope echoing softly within the flooded cabin of your heart. "When you pass through the waters, I will be with you, and through the rivers, they will not overwhelm you. For I am your Captain, and am calling you to this journey across troubled waters. Yes it is true, there are many obstacles hindering your progress. Yet knowing this, I called you, and am calling you still. Come; come with Me to the other side."

Your body shivers from the extreme cold as you cling tightly to your vessel's floating debris. Surrounded by miles of indigo blue, your fears are laid to rest beneath the living waters, as you trust in Him. His waves of peace billow gently about you, bringing warmth to your soul. And you find strength in the current of His love.

The cloudless sky is ablaze with millions of twinkling points of light. Radiant beams can be seen dotting the distant horizon, casting a warm glow upon the still waters. Land ho! Your unscheduled delay is now but a memory as you drift slowly towards the illuminated shore. The waters of your heart's cabin have receded. Excitement wells up within you. And with it flows the hope and dream of a brighter tomorrow.

OBEDIENCE. WHEN GOD says to do something, we must be like *Nike*, and just do it. And we must do so promptly. To take a line from a sermon I once heard, "to delay is to disobey and to disobey is not okay." *The Interrupted Life* was written after completing a Bible study on Jonah, as a personal reminder to obey.

"Has the Lord as great delight in burnt offerings and sacrifices, as in obeying the voice of the Lord? Behold, to obey is better than sacrifice, and to heed than the fat of rams. For rebellion is as the sin of witchcraft, and stubbornness is as iniquity and idolatry."
(1 Samuel 15:22-23)

"He also taught me, and said to me: 'Let your heart retain my words; keep my commands and live. Get wisdom! Get understanding! Do not forget, nor turn away from the words of my mouth. Do not forsake her, and she will preserve you; love her and she will keep you. Wisdom is the principal thing; therefore get wisdom. And in all your getting, get understanding."
(Proverbs 4:4-7)

THE INTERRUPTED LIFE

You've paid your fare and are ready to set sail upon tranquil seas. Seeking a respite from life's pressing problems, you embark upon this unexpected journey to a paradise of sorts. However, this excursion is no pleasure cruise. There are no welcoming crews to greet and attend your every need. An events calendar has not been placed in your room, neither are there courtesy calls alerting you of any schedule changes. No, the only reminder you have is from the ship's Captain. You know, the one you received in your confirmation e-mail. The one that sent you on a dead run in the opposite direction. The reason you find yourself being the sole passenger aboard this intrepid vessel – *The Interrupted Life.*

Unfortunately, there aren't a lot of distractions aboard this exclusive ocean liner. No games, activities, nor any arts and entertainment. There isn't even a resident masseuse standing ready to relieve your tired muscles. Though appetizing enough, the cuisine on this craft is hardly palatable for a mutinous heart. Servings of surrender, faithfulness and obedience are offered on the menu. And you kind of lost your appetite for those delicacies awhile back. So you bypass the meal plan, for now anyway. And while you packed appropriate cruise wear for the trip, there are no attendants to launder your dirty apparel. For the ship's bitter waters fail to cleanse your soiled attire, much less your errant heart. And like your clothing, your spiritual odor is both foul and a bit offensive. Yet still, you sail on.

Crashing waves torment the walls of your vessel on every side. The oscillating motion, you know, the rising feelings of guilt, rock you back and forth, upsetting your nerves and quelling your ebbing resolve. And you become physically ill from all the commotion.

More troubling than rough waters, however, are the sounds, or more importantly, the heightened lack thereof. Whereas before that still, small voice was like soothing music to your soul, its deafening silence now drowns out your heart's cries for peace. How you wish you could return to those carefree days when you walked with a bounce in your step and a song in your heart. When your shoulders were not weighed down with shame. For the intense heat of conviction slowly simmers, crowning your brow with beads of regret. Though you didn't verbally disobey the Captain's orders, your actions conveyed non-compliance just the same. For like an Olympic runner, you sprinted. Your actions a nonverbal response, quite similar, in fact, to that of another marathon traveler. Perhaps you've heard of him.

Jonah, too, ran from God's will and was shipwrecked on the seas of disobedience. Instructed to "arise and go," he journeyed far; but like you, in the opposite direction. His defiance eventually found him sandwiched between layers of salty seaweed. Smothered in slime, he was served up as the main dish on rebellion's seafood platter. Where he lost his appetite for fugitive living. Funny, how a different perspective is often gained in isolation. For wisdom is enlightened in hindsight. And with wisdom, comes understanding. Jonah realized it was either God's way or the highway . . . or in his case, under the seaway. Like a shining beacon, that morsel of truth guided that wayward runner back to freedom. And his subsequent obedience changed a nation.

So, how about you? Are you ready to be released to be all, do all and see all that the Lord has purposed for you? For He is not interested in your vain attempts to make amends, your valiant vows of service, your heartfelt promises of sacrifice. They fall flat anyway, much like a fallen soufflé. No, the Lord God does not delight in sacrifices. It is your obedience that pleases Him. And if you love Him, you'll obey Him.

A shrill whistle signals the journey's end. Glistening waters ripple gently upon the approaching shoreline, while radiant rays poke through flowing rivers of mist. Surveying your surroundings, you are surprised to behold a familiar landmark. For despite your deliberate diversion, you are once again at your original port of call. And you cry tears of gratitude and praise. For this ship's Officer, your Heavenly Father, is a God of Second Chances.

So arise and go and be at peace. For your Skipper stands ready to navigate your life through unchartered territory. Though the skies ahead may be overcast, He is more than able to guide you safely to your destination. For when you pass through troubled waters, they will not overwhelm you. And through the fog of adversity, you will not be hindered. For He is with you and He loves you. So go now, savoring the fresh breeze upon your face as you look with expectation towards the future. Breathe in the hope of new life as you step out in faith. And believe, for you are not alone. Your unseen companion is none other than the Creator of the Universe. And He's got your back.

Now may the blessings and favor of the Lord be upon you as your journey traverses the billowy seas of life. Oh, and don't forget to check your Holy Almanac for travel updates . . . lest you again find yourself an unwitting passenger aboard *The Interrupted Life*.

TRANSITION. JUST AS in labor and delivery, transition in life can oftentimes be painful. I can remember where I was when the following piece was written. For the first time in my life, I was in a position of leadership. Our church was in the middle of extended revival meetings, and yet I still maintained the kid's busy activities schedule, all the while not missing a service. After the last carpool run, I would hurry the children to the church where they would sit quietly doing their homework.

My attempts at being "Supermom" came to an abrupt halt after my friend, Anne, noticing how frazzled I was looking, simply posed the following question. "Why do you go to church so much?" For the life of me, I don't know what my response would have been had not that still, small voice caution me to think before answering. Maybe she wasn't expecting an answer, for my evasion merely allowed her opportunity to segue seamlessly into a new conversation. A couple of days later, I found myself sitting in front of my computer when her question resurfaced in my mind. My immediate response startled me – "because that was what was expected of me." It was at that moment that I realized I had become what Jesus hated. Religious. I had been active in church to be seen by and receive the praise of men. And so I stepped down from everything ministry-related, with the purpose of seeking God for what He would have me do. Outwardly, this submission precipitated years of personal inactivity. But then only God knows what goes on *Behind Closed Doors*.

"Most assuredly I say to you, unless a grain of wheat falls into the ground and dies, it remains alone; but if it dies, it produces much grain."
(John 12:24)

"For the word of God is living and powerful, and sharper than any two-edged sword, piercing even to the division of soul and spirit, and joints and marrow, and is a discerner of the thoughts and intents of the heart."
(Hebrews 4:12)

"But let patience have its perfect work, that you may be perfect and complete, lacking nothing."
(James 1:4)

Behind Closed Doors

A few years ago, there was a popular song that received a great deal of airplay on the radio - *Behind Closed Doors*. A line from its chorus was "No one knows what goes on behind closed doors." This was, of course, regarding the bedroom of a married couple, but can have spiritual connotations as well.

All seems to be right in your world. Your walk with the Lord is at an invigorating, steady pace. Your heart is light and turned towards Him. There is great evidence of His working in and through you. When suddenly, He calls you to walk upon a different pathway. The road ahead seems less traveled, unpaved. Each new step takes you further away from life as you have known it. And you are out of your comfort zone, unsettled, ill at ease.

On this journey, the skies of your life become overcast, as you try to find your way through the heavy mist. Several times you lose your footing, yet you continue onward. The fog lifts revealing an open door. Walking through the threshold, you hear it close firmly behind you. You try repeatedly to open it, but it appears locked from the outside. And then you know. There is no turning back. For no matter how hard one may struggle, one can never open a door that has been shut by the hand of God. So like Noah, you feel shut in, as the rains begin to fall.

The sudden downburst brings a change in your ministry, as you are placed upon the Shelf of Preparation. One by one, you begin to lay aside the many works to which you felt called. No longer do you feel it necessary to do what others expect of you. Family, friends and co-workers do not understand you. Even fellow-Believers question your uncharacteristic behavior. Whereas before you would have felt the need to justify your actions, this time you do not. Instead you do as Mary did, telling no one of God's plans for you, pondering them in your heart. For it is written, *"Blessed is she who believed, for there will be a fulfillment of those things told her from the Lord."*

Then comes a change in your relationships. Your circle of friends has become smaller. Even those closest to you have become merely acquaintances. Realizing their importance in your life is greater than God intended, you pull back. Though you are gripped with pangs of loneliness, you remain hopeful that some may accompany you at your journey's end. Meanwhile the ground beneath you gives way to the swelling waters, and you drift further away from all that is familiar.

Most remarkable, however, is the change in you. While you cannot put your finger on exactly when and how this change occurred, the difference is noticeable. Where frustration used to give in to anger, it now lies down in acceptance. Once long-term residents, hurt feelings are now overnight guests. Bitterness no longer flows from a cistern brimming with polluted waters, as mercy and grace pour from your lips. Eyes that look back at you in the mirror give only a hint of the transformation within. All the while you wonder where this spiritual metamorphosis will lead.

Gale-force winds of change scatter the leaves of your life, leaving your limbs bare. The air turns bitter cold and you feel naked, exposed and alone. It is a winter season in your life. What once was fertile now seems barren. Hopes, dreams, desires have fallen off the tree of your life and been carried away with the winds. Your life is a maze of brokenness. Broken dreams, broken relationships, a broken heart, a broken will. Still, you continue to sit upon the now dusty shelf, while the floodwaters continue to rise.

At times you feel restless, without purpose. Normal is no longer normal as you go about with what you consider to be menial tasks. As the desire to do a great work still burns like kindling in your heart, you become frustrated with the mundane. For after many years of serving, you feel this time on the shelf to be wasted, idle time. Nothing, however, could be further from the truth. *For to everything there is a season, a time for every purpose under the sun.* And this is your time of preparation.

Can you not see the "Under Construction" sign posted along the scaffolding of your heart's exterior? For a major renovation is going on behind this spiritual veil. Walls are being torn down, hidden motivations are being stripped and varnished. Wrong beliefs are being pulled up and replaced with seeds of truth. Long-forgotten hurts and grievances are being brought to the surface and swept away. Priorities are being reset, as a new vision is being formed in you. Just as the formation of a child takes place in the secret of its mother's womb, so is what is being done in you. For the Lord is doing a deep work, a thorough work, within your heart.

So, be not discouraged. For one day, as in the days of Noah, the waters will recede, and God's rainbow will again adorn your skies. His hand will unlock the doors, releasing you into all He has prepared for you. Your heart will be light; your spirit refreshed, your soul at peace, as you resume your walk upon the pathway of His choosing. Until then, you must wait. Wait patiently upon Him as He completes what He has begun in private. Behind closed doors.

And no one knows what goes on behind closed doors.

AWAKENINGS. THERE ARE times when our senses are invigorated, made alive with the wonder of an awesome God. With my little one sleeping peacefully in his stroller, my friend Tracee and I were sharing testimonies while sitting on a brightly painted wooden bench in a children's park. It was a clear summer day, one that afforded us opportunity to view the Sierra Mountains framing the horizon. The lightness of her spirit and the spontaneous joy that exuded from her was so refreshing, giving this glass half-empty kind of girl a new perspective. Using a diaper bag as a portable desk, *Sweet Serenity* was written amidst the happy sounds of children playing beneath a cloudless afternoon sky.

And let the beauty of the Lord our God be upon us."
(Psalm 90:17)

Sweet Serenity

There is a sweet serenity
A stillness in my soul
A peace that comes from healing
The joy of being whole.

A gentle breeze is blowing
The clouds have gone away
My Savior's arms enfold me
And there I want to stay.

He covers me with His feathers
Hides me safely within His wings
I bask in the warmth of His love
As He shows me glorious things.

The wonder of the heavens
Beauty of the star-kissed skies
Mountain peaks and rolling valleys
His handiwork in nature lies.

The calmness all around me
My heart begins to sing
The song of adoration
As I worship the King of Kings.

CONNECTIONS. BEING ABLE to connect anywhere, anyplace, anytime, is convenient, but leaves little time to quiet one's thoughts. Intended to make life easier, today's high tech society instead adds to the already surmounting pressures of life. And yet, God does not expect us to work ourselves into exhaustion. Sometimes He calls us to rest, to reconnect with Him. *Rest In Me* was His song of rest to me.

"Come aside by yourselves to a deserted place and rest a while."
(Mark 6:31)

REST IN ME

Rest in Me
My beloved
Rest in Me
I am calling you to rest
Rest in Me
Lay aside
Your cares, your burdens
Cast away
Your fears, your worries
Enter in
Find your rest
Rest in Me

SOMETIMES WE JUST have to take a moment, lay down our cares and responsibilities and find strength and renewal in our Father's arms. While reflecting on a former President's informal addresses to the nation, I likened them to having conversations with God. *Fireside Chat* was a result of that contemplation.

"Call to Me, and I will answer you, and show you great and mighty things, which you do not know."
(Jeremiah 33:3)

FIRESIDE CHAT

A few years ago our television screens were lit up with warm, homespun images - a cardigan sweater, an overstuffed armchair, a crackling fire in a marble fireplace. The setting was The White House, and President Carter was inviting us to join him in a fireside chat. Wanting to bring the people of the nation, as if we were one big, happy family into his living room, he shared with us his plans, his goals for the future of our country.

Though the media and other critics ridiculed him, calling his efforts simple, reflecting on his attempts years later, one can grasp the wisdom in its simplicity. And really is it not the simple things that count in life, the little things that touch us, that warm our hearts? A rainbow arching the skies after a spring rain. A gentle breeze as it caresses your face on a hot, summer day. The pride in your children's eyes as they hand you a bouquet picked from among flowering weeds. And the joy that you feel as you watch them sleeping peacefully in their beds. Simple, yet little things, that if we are too busy, may slip by unnoticed.

For our world today turns at such a hectic pace. Exerting ourselves making preparations for tomorrow, we oftentimes fail to enjoy today. Life's burdens and responsibilities weigh heavily upon us so that at times we find ourselves going in directions opposite of our spouses, meeting only briefly as we fall wearily into our beds. And before drifting off to sleep, we wonder if life was meant to be this way. Busily providing for the future, while the present slips quietly into the past.

And then there are our children. With so many work and social obligations, guilt sets into our hearts and we try to ease our consciences with excessive gift giving. Closets, shelves and toy boxes overflow with peace offerings bought with our hard-earned dollars. Empty trinkets of our affection; when what they really want is our time, is our love. But we are caught up on society's ever-spinning merry-go-round; and so we continue onward, going in circles.

And then suddenly the winds of change blow into our lives. The cool breeze whips into our schedules, upsetting them. Nature's elements cut off our connection to the outside world, overturning our lives as we struggle making adjustments.

Seasoned wood is placed in our fireplaces. The warmth of dancing flames almost hypnotic, inviting us to come and sit a spell, and we toss pillows in front of the open hearth. Strategically placed candles create a welcome ambience, an atmosphere for conversation, as we begin sharing with one another our hopes and dreams, reminiscing on days gone by. And as we do, we make new memories, treasured moments to be enjoyed again and again in years to come. How we welcome this uninvited interlude. Snuggling between quilts and blankets, our bodies are not the only things that are warmed. Our hearts are warmed as a bond is made between us. For the frigid winds of change have somehow brought with them warmth, causing us to spend time with one another.

You know, God in Heaven is like that, too. So many times we are so busy serving others, trying to do good deeds in life, that we neglect the One who gave us life. Yes, He wants us to do for others; but like our children, He also longs to spend quality time with us. Like them, He misses us when we go about our days with scarcely a thought, barely a word for Him. And though we try to fill our squares carrying out our Sunday and/or mid-week church obligations, it does little to lessen the pain within His heart. For instead of living full lives as He intended, we merely exist in busy, fragmented ones. And when the day is done, our energies spent, we find ourselves drained and empty. Yet hovering over us, as a mother over her child, God reaches down kissing our weary hearts goodnight. And though we notice the peace that settles upon us, we do not acknowledge its source; and we close our eyes for a much-needed sleep.

So, the next time a gentle wind caresses your face, think of Him.

Think of your Heavenly Father calling you to come and sit with Him in front of a cozy fire. Be warmed as He shares loving thoughts from His heart to yours. And as you do, thank Him. Thank Him for your blessings, your life, your family, and enjoy every precious moment together. For He came that we might have a full and satisfying life.

Put another log on the fire, and like our former President, settle your heart down for a warm fireside chat.

LIFE'S CHAOS OFTEN drowns out the Spirit's soft whisper to quiet ourselves and come away with Him. But isn't it amazing how much clearer our thoughts and lives can become when we do? *A Cup of Christmas Tea* was written when my seemingly endless "holiday to do" list screamed for my attention.

"Behold! I stand at the door and knock. If anyone hears my voice and opens the door, I will come in to him and dine with him, and he with Me."
(Revelation 3:20)

"But seek first the kingdom of God and his righteousness, and all these things shall be added to you."
(Matthew 6:33)

A Cup of Christmas Tea

Rising twin loaves of Sourdough Bread filled the house with an intoxicating aroma. A flaky Cinnamon Apple Crumb Pie cooled on the wire rack atop the countertop. Mixed with spices from the homemade chili simmering on the stove, her home was a warm invitation for communion. All the while a roaring fire in the wood-burning fireplace added to the welcome ambience.

It was the night after Christmas. The presents had been opened, some of the contents proudly displayed throughout the house. The turkey had been carved and eaten, the leftovers wrapped and given to dinner guests. Many a well wish had been sent and received. Some of which were penned in the cards strung across the evergreen garland draping the staircase. The fragrance of the season lingered as holiday favorites played softly in the background. Walking past the room where her children were making nice with their toys, she pauses on the stairs to peruse the card's heartfelt sentiments. Taking a deep breath, she closes her eyes and sighs.

All seemed right in her world, but then appearances can be deceiving. Placing her arms about herself, she shivers from the cold. Not the cold outside, for her home was warmed by the Yule logs burning in the fireplace. No, this cold was on the inside, inside her heart. For all was not well with her soul.

Regret soured like unripe grapes within a heart pressed with disappointment. For Christmas had come and gone; and once again she was left with a feeling of emptiness, a feeling of loss. Those restless feelings began around Black Friday; the biggest shopping day of the year. With each passing day, she found herself becoming more and more frustrated with the season and it's commercialism.

For harried shoppers poured out their hard-earned wages as one would a glass of lukewarm water - without a second thought. Shop vendors enticed buyers with bargains advertised as too good to be true. Bargains that no one should be without, that would later be returned the day after Christmas. She had, herself, stood in line earlier that morning returning such a bargain. And none of it, she thought, none of it, had anything to do with the true meaning of the season.

Looking out the frosted windowpanes, she catches sight of her reflection in the beveled glass. Though this was the season to be jolly, sorrow returned its gaze from eyes peering intently through puffs of mist into the darkness. The stars in the sky twinkled their melodic evensong, contrary to the one echoing within her heart. A heart now made heavy with regret.

"Lord," she whispers, "all I wanted this year was to truly honor the real meaning of Christmas in my heart. I did not want to get caught up in the season's traditional trappings, the frantic activity and the holiday rush. I wanted it to be a special time where, like the wise men of old, my heart would embark upon a spiritual journey, one that would allow me to share with others the true joy of the season. But as in years past, despite my good intentions, my efforts were no different than those of the commercial world about me. And now that it's all over, I have to ask myself. What was it all for? I am exhausted from the frenzy of getting ready for Christmas."

So deep were her thoughts that she failed to notice the figure coming up her walkway. Unaware of his presence, she continued her inward contemplation. The sudden rapping of the doorknocker startles her. She throws open the door without glancing through the peephole. A man of average height stood before her. Simply dressed, he wore a heavy wool coat over clean, faded blue jeans. A knit scarf covered most of his face. With worn leather-gloved hands, he gently takes her smaller ones into his own. Gazing into his eyes, she senses a familiarity. Though from what she could see, his face was unfamiliar. Without thinking, she invites him into her home for a cup of Christmas tea.

Putting the kettle on the stove and getting her finest china from the rosewood cabinet in the dining room, she heads back towards the breakfast area where her guest has made himself comfortable.

His scarf and coat are draped neatly over the back of the overstuffed recliner in the adjoining family room. Bending over the fireplace, he warms his scarred hands over the roaring fire. The thought occurs to her that it seemed quite natural for him to be there.

The scent of ground cloves and cinnamon mingle with those of the chili and fresh bread now cooling on the kitchen counter. It is an enticing aroma. As she approaches the table, she stumbles, upsetting the delicate china. They shatter into hundreds of tiny pieces upon the tiled floor. Embarrassed, she buries her flushed face in her hands, as frustration again wells up within her.

"Allow me to get that for you," offers the stranger, as he locates the broom and dustpan in the laundry room next to the kitchen. For a moment she wonders how he knew where to find them.

Sweeping up the broken pieces of porcelain, he attempts to put at ease the frazzled mind of his gracious hostess.

"Do not be troubled. You fret over broken china. You worry yourself with regrets. But I ask you. Why is your soul cast down, and why are you disquieted within? Is your hope not in God? Broken pieces of clay can be easily replaced. But a broken heart is not easily mended."

He stoops down to retrieve what looks to be the remnants of a cup's handle, and then continues.

"I have heard your heart's cry, my child. Like this broken cup handle, you must choose carefully which traditions you will hold onto, and which you will throw away. It is true many choose to celebrate the season in ways that have nothing to do with its real meaning, but what has that to do with you? Regardless of what others do, you must honor Christmas in your heart, keeping it the whole year through. For as you do, others will see and desire the joy they see in you."

Emptying the fragments into the wastebasket, he continues. "And the emptiness you feel inside will be filled. Hope will again find it's home within you. So release your cares and allow the sweetness of my presence to envelop you. For in my presence is fullness of joy."

Pouring the tea into earthenware mugs found in the kitchen cabinet, he settles down in a cushioned chair next to hers. They do not speak; yet instead savor the tea, the moment and each other's company.

"Precious daughter," he says softly, "rest in the peace that comes with my presence. Enjoy the life you have been given. And enjoy me as I enjoy you."

The smile that lit up her face mirrored the brilliant flames in the open hearth. A feeling of peace envelops her, as she realizes the identity of the one sharing this intimate moment with her. And she drops to her knees in holy reverence.

"Oh Lord," she cries. "Who am I that you should come and visit me? I am not worthy of such an honor."

Shaking his head, he smiles. Reaching down, he gently lifts her to her feet. With great tenderness, he gazes pensively into the very windows to her soul, and dries her tears.

"Mary did not feel worthy of the honor bestowed upon her either," he reminisces, "but like her, Dear One, you, too, are highly favored. And as she surrendered her all to the Father, letting go of her preconceived ideas, her plans, her hopes, her dreams, so must you. In so doing, just like Mary, great shall be your reward. For our Father rewards those who diligently seek Him."

Gathering his things from the recliner, he heads toward the front door.

"Thank you for the tea, my daughter. It was as warm and inviting as your heart lying open before me. Though you may not see me again for a while, do not be discouraged. Instead take the time each day to cease from your doings and quiet yourself with a cup of tea. Not only is it refreshing for your body, but the quiet time will be refreshment for your spirit as well. And as you drink of the cup, remember me. Remember our time together. Remember I am with you always. Remember I love you."

Delicate ice crystals continue their weightless descent. She watches him as he walks down her now-covered sidewalk. Between a light mist and the falling snow, he disappears into the starry night. She breathes a sigh of contentment for what was lost was now found; what was empty was now filled. Closing the door to the chill winter air, she is warmed as hope again burns brightly within her.

And may it be so with us as we honor the Reason for the Season in our hearts today and every day. Spreading joy to the world for the Lord has surely come.

Homemade chili simmers on the stove. Miniature lights flash in time to a familiar carol playing softly on the radio. The happy bantering of children fills her heart and home with joy and laughter. It is the night after Christmas and all is well. All is well with her soul.

EVERY YEAR THE world pauses on December 25th to have a celebration. Homes are decorated, feasts are prepared and gifts are exchanged. And yet in most of those gatherings, the guest of honor is hardly mentioned, much less invited.

I can remember when my eldest, Veronica, was a toddler. Being the only child at the time, a mountain of presents bearing her name surrounded the Christmas tree. Her eyes grew wide with excitement, as each new treasure was unwrapped. But then a strange thing happened. Midway through opening her mass of gifts, she grew tired and put them aside. It was a moment that made me consider whose birthday it was anyway. *The Birthday Party* was written the following year.

"For God so loved the world that He gave His only begotten Son, that whosoever believes in Him should not perish but have everlasting life. For God did not send His Son into the world to condemn the world, but that the world through Him might be saved."
(John 3:16-17)

THE BIRTHDAY PARTY

I went to my birthday party
Although no one knew I was there
So I found a place in a corner
Sat down in a rocking chair.

My children had gathered together
With friends and family
To celebrate my birthday
Inviting everyone but Me.

As I sat alone in that chair in the corner
Observing the festivities
I knew that my birthday party
Was not as it should be.

For they had brought in many idols
And if you rearrange carefully
The letters of their Christmas god
You'll have the name of my enemy.

But even so, I still do love them
More than words could ever say
Yet I wish that they would honor Me
In a different kind of way.

For it seems their celebration
Has become commercialized
A moneymaking world event
If only they realized.

That Christmas is not in buying
Gifts on others to impart
But is in giving a gift that money can't buy
It's a love matter of the heart.

For God so loved the world
He came to set the captives free
Made a way for them to live with Him
For all eternity.

More than a baby in a manger
Born on a starry night
But God Incarnate became man
To earth was brought great light.

Yet through the years this message
Of my coming has gotten lost
More valuable than silver
Precious souls are being lost.

For when I look upon their faces
I see pain and frustration there
Their shoulders are heavy with burdens
Their hearts are filled with cares.

It seems they have forgotten
That I came so they may be
Living a life that's rich and full
A life more abundantly.

And as I looked at all the presents
Underneath the Christmas tree
The tears began to fill my eyes
For one was left for Me.

I arose to seek my treasure
The gift that bore my name
And upon opening I found a note
What it said made me glad I came.

"With eyes to see and ears to hear
And a heart that is open wide
Please, Lord Jesus, enter in
My heart, come and abide."

And from that little gesture
I knew that I was welcome there
I knew I had been invited
Knew that somebody cared.

My beloved ones, I ask of you
Please open up your heart
And let me come abide with you
Nevermore to be apart.

So I go now to another party
Looking for somebody to
Say "Happy Birthday, Dear Jesus"
Could that someone be you?

I REMEMBER WALKING the streets of a busy metropolitan city during the holidays and observing a scattering of people seeking meals from overstuffed trash bins. It was a sobering moment, for but for the grace of God that could have been me. For situations and wrong choices could place any one of us on the streets, searching for food, a place to stay, for assistance. And though our hearts are stirred to help, we oftentimes don't know where to begin. *Silver and Gold* was my heart's realization that sharing the Father's love in practical ways was a good place to start.

"And a certain man lame from his mother's womb was carried, whom they laid daily at the gate of the temple which is called Beautiful, to ask alms from those who entered the temple; who, seeing Peter and John about to go into the temple, asked for alms. And fixing his eyes on him, with John, Peter said, 'Look at us.' So he gave them his attention, expecting to receive something from them. Then Peter said, 'Silver and gold I do not have, but what I do have I give you: In the name of Jesus Christ of Nazareth, rise up and walk.' And he took him by the right hand and lifted him up, and immediately his feet and ankle bones received strength."
(Acts 3:2-7)

Silver and Gold

Warmed by a cozy fire
They gathered 'round the Christmas tree
With hearts full of thanksgiving
Bearing gifts honoring Me.

Exchanging love-wrapped packages
Sharing memories
Spending time together
With special friends and family.

Yet outside their walls on city streets
Live others not so blessed
Whose spirits have been broken
Whose lives have been oppressed.

They are the walking wounded
Outcasts of society
Conveniently forgotten
In a depressed economy.

Reduced to live like paupers
Though at one time, some lived like kings
Yet somehow circumstances
Caused them to all lose everything.

And as I walked the streets unseen by men
I heard a heart-rending cry
"God, why did you let this happen
It's so unfair, please let me die."

With hair unkempt and tattered clothes
his hands clenched in a fist
"Dear One," I whispered softly
"I did not create your life for this.

For I Am Jehovah-Jireh
Your provider, let Me be
Oh the riches I have stored for you
For all eternity.

But you must put your trust in Me
For only I can give to you
A way in which to meet your needs
Make broken dreams come true."

But his heart was hard and seared by pain
And my words he did not hear
Held in bondage by oppression
His eyes blinded by his tears.

As I peered into the darkened hearts
Walking the dim-lit streets
I saw a ray of light, my chosen one
And made plans for them to meet.

"Precious Daughter," I spoke to her heart
"See the hungry, hear their cries
See the wounded one before you
Read his plea for help upon that sign."

"Will work for food to feed my family
God bless you as you give
Anything you can
Will make it easier for us to live."

She looked into his hollow eyes
Saw his need and felt his hurt
Placed both her arms around him
Looking past the stench and dirt.

"Silver and gold, I do not have," she said
"But what I have, I give to you
An introduction to the One
Who can make your broken dreams come true.

Please come and bring your family
I know a place where you can eat
A home-cooked Christmas dinner
Gather your things now, come with me."

And throughout the meal she spoke the words
My heart longed to convey
And within his heart a spark was lit
The hope of a brighter day.

The tears welled up within his eyes
For his heart had grasped the truth
That in his own frail human strength
He'd done all that he could do.

And could it be this was the answer
What more was there to lose
And so with eyes towards Heaven
Eternal riches he did choose.

The road ahead may not be easy
But I Am He who holds the key
To unlock the doors before him
Barred by society.

But there are many others like him
Cold and lonely on the streets
Will you be my chosen one
I need for them to meet?

Will you share with them the bread of life
That never will go stale
Will you give a cup of water
Drawn from my living well?

How my heart is grieved within me
Because they cannot see
Beyond their circumstances
That I alone am what they need.

Warming their hands around the fire
In trash barrels on the streets
The destitute and lonely
Needing refuge, needing Me.

THE PRINCESS BRIDE was written as an encouragement from The Bridegroom to one of his beloved brides, experiencing repercussions due to the indiscretions of a loved one.

"Like a lily among thorns, so is my love among the daughters."
(Song of Solomon 2:2)

"My beloved spoke and said to me: 'Rise up, my love, my fair one, and come away. For lo, the winter is past, the rain is over and gone. The flowers appear on the earth; the time of singing has come, and the voice of the turtledove is heard in our land'."
(Song of Solomon 2:10-12)

"Many waters cannot quench love, nor can the floods drown it."
(Song of Solomon 8:7)

THE PRINCESS BRIDE

Arise, my love, my fair one
Arise, come away with Me
Life's bitter winter
Cold and harsh
Is but a memory

Rains of abuse, gale winds of torment
Blizzards of fear, rejection, pain
That ravaged your heart
Tilled its' fallow ground
Have yielded a garden buffet

For lo, the winter is past
The rains over and gone
The flowers have begun to bloom
Hear the song that your heart now is singing
The love song of your Ravished Bridegroom

Who is she who looks forth as the morning
Fair as the moon, clear and pure as the sun
Come to Me that I may look upon you
Fairest of women
Chosen One

For with one look of your eyes
You have captured My heart
Through life's testing to Me you've been true
No water can quench nor darkness hide
The flame of love that burns brightly for you

For like the maiden barefoot by the cinders
Oppressed in life filled with drudgery
Mistreated
By those you have trusted
One enslaved has become royalty

And I long to crown you with honor and glory
Adorn you in My righteousness
Give you slippers of peace
For your weary feet
And a scepter of faithfulness

Oh how lovely you are, how lovely
Like a lily among thorns are you
Do you long that I eat of the fruit of your garden
My heart seeks an answer
Say "I do"

So come away, my beloved, my fair one
To the mountains of spice
We will ride
Ascending the heights of pure godly desire
Arise; come away with Me, my Princess Bride

THE AIRPORT WAS filled with travelers and I don't remember whom I was dropping off that morning. But shortly afterwards, I noticed a young woman crying in one of the seating areas in the terminal. It seems her boyfriend had deserted her and she needed money to get home. Our church was in the middle of revival meetings so I not only took her home with me, but also to the remaining services that week. Not only did the congregation buy her plane ticket home, but she also found never-ending love as she met and gave her heart to the Lord.

Out of that seemingly chance, yet divine meeting, came *No Crib For A Bed*.

"I have been young, and now am old; yet I have not seen the righteous forsaken, nor his descendants begging bread."
(Psalm 37:25)

"Even the sparrow has found a home, and the swallow a nest for herself, where she may lay her young – even Your altars, O Lord of hosts, my King and my God."
(Psalm 84:3)

No Crib For A Bed

Standing before the locked door of her studio apartment, tears streamed down the young woman's face. Posted on the peeling wood was an eviction notice. Scattered about the dimly lit hallway were her meager belongings. 'Twas the season of goodwill toward men, yet fellow residents offered no holiday greetings. Though their hearts were stirred to help, they knew well enough not to get involved. Any attempts to make the landlord change his mind could result in their rents being raised should they interfere. And so they passed her by. She would have to find a new place to live, for there was no room for her here.

For days she wandered crowded streets seeking refuge. With each passing day, her clothes became more tattered and worn. Her unwashed body reeked of sweat. Her face bore the faint markings of abuse. She was weary from the pressures of life.

Suddenly, a sharp pain pierces her swollen belly. Wincing, she leans against a storefront wall until the pain subsides. Her mind begins to race frantically, wondering if the child she carries is about to be born. Another contraction quickly follows confirming her fears. It is time. Eyeing a soiled mattress in the adjacent alley, she heads for and gently lowers herself upon the throwaway bed. For the next few moments she is alone. Alone with her thoughts. Alone with her labor. Alone.

"Oh God," she prays, "everyone tried to warn me, but I wouldn't listen. I thought he loved me." She absently traces her fingers over a fading scar, a painful reminder of his true affections toward her. "Please help me. I don't know what to do."

Startled by a sudden noise near the overflowing dumpsters, she turns and finds herself staring into the eyes of a black Doberman. His gaze is dark and menacing, yet for some reason she is unafraid. He glides toward her, circles the mattress and lies down at her side. Seized by another contraction she moans aloud, while the dog softly whimpers, licking her hand in comfort.

"Max," a voice calls out. "Max, here boy!"

The animal barks, yet does not leave the pregnant woman's side. A middle-aged woman, dressed in holiday wear, and carrying a bouquet of roses and pine leaves, enters the alleyway. Her brow furrows as she assesses the gravity of the situation. Kneeling down, she carefully helps the young woman to her feet.

"Oh, Sweetie, let me help you," she begins. "My husband and I own a neighborhood grocery store right around the corner. If you'll come with me, there's a room in the back. It's not much; but it's comfortable. I sometimes sleep there myself; especially during our quarterly inventory."

Small, but clean, the room held an antique double bed, an old-fashioned dresser, a pair of nesting tables and a solid oak rocking chair. A mural, depicting nature in winter, adorned the walls, giving the room a peaceful ambience. Placing the flowers in a crystal vase on one of the tables, she quickly turns back the covers of a goose down comforter and fluffs the two oversized pillows. Emptying one of the cupboards of its contents, she carefully lines it with various strips of quilted fabric found in the storeroom.

The young woman was moaning softly now, as beads of perspiration mingle with the silent tears flowing down her face. This was not how she imagined her child would be born. In the back of a grocery store, attended by a strange woman, sporting a seasonal hat, and a curious dog pacing back and forth at the foot of a stranger's bed.

The cry of a newborn resounded loudly in the small quarters. A cry so tender, its innocence pierced the heart of this modern-day Good Samaritan. She thought of her own daughter and grandson living overseas on a military installation. This would be their first Christmas apart. And oh how she missed them. Wrapping the tiny babe in a soft blanket and placing him in the cloth-lined drawer, she begins quietly humming a traditional carol.

Customers, hearing of the baby born in the store's backroom, appeared bringing gifts for the child, as well as nightclothes and toiletries for the young mother. Some even gave monetary provisions that might meet not only their needs, but some of their wants as well. While looking upon the young family, all were reminded of another birth over 2,000 years ago. And they wondered if this child, too, would grow into greatness.

Rocking back and forth in the comfortable rocker, the fresh scent of pine permeating the room, the young woman is overwhelmed by this spontaneous outpouring of affection. Away from family and friends in her time of trouble, strangers had appeared bearing gifts – offerings of comfort and joy. These unexpected acts of kindness restored not only her faith in mankind, but had solidified her hope in the Living God. For the birth of her child had brought her new life. Closing her eyes, she thanked the Lord for answered prayer while a holiday lullaby began flowing from the depths of a grateful heart.

"Away in a manger, no crib for a bed."

The visitors hovering about the doorway joined in the chorus. Hearts and voices blended together, while, from the tile floor, ebony eyes kept watch over the little one sleeping peacefully in an antique dresser drawer.

This year while many hearts are pregnant, expectant with the hope of Christmas, there are countless others barren of the joy the holidays bring. May we listen for and quiet their cries by extending goodwill toward our fellow man. For from the lowliest of men to the world's greatest king, the song of the season is to be sung by all of God's children.

"Bless all the dear children in your tender care. And take us to heaven to live with you there."

No VACANCY. MARY and Joseph were turned away with those words as they sought shelter that starry night in Bethlehem. Spiritually, we are all in need of refuge. There is, however, room in God's heart for everyone. We only need call upon Him; He will not turn us away. And so, may our hearts be a manger as we make room for Him, not only at Christmas, but the whole year through. *No Room In The Inn* was written one year after watching a children's holiday special with my kids.

"And she brought forth her firstborn Son, and wrapped Him in swaddling cloths, and laid Him in a manger, because there was no room for them in the inn."
(Luke 2:7)

"The Lord is not slack concerning His promise, as some count slackness, but is longsuffering toward us, not willing that any should perish but that all should come to repentance."
(2 Peter 3:9)

No Room In The Inn

Ponder these thoughts for a moment
Meditate on them, my friend
Is your heart a crowded manger
Your life a busy inn?

Are your swaddling cloths cares and worries
Keeping you wrapped up, with no peace within
Void of time to enjoy life's treasures
Simple pleasures with family and friends?

Then take heart for the Lord desires
You enjoy all that's been given you
Yet you must cease now from all of your strivings
For where have they gotten you.

Days and nights spent constantly doing
Frantically running about to and fro
Like the little lab mice in their cages
Running in circles, with no place to go.

And like the innkeeper who cried "We have no room"
When God beckons what is your reply
"My schedule is busy, my calendar's full
There's no room, I just don't have the time."

But there was another He beckoned that evening
In the small town of Bethlehem
Who made a home for Him in a stable
For there was no room for Him in the inn.

And while his eyes beheld his treasure
Along with others who'd journeyed to see
The skies were lit up by the heavenly hosts
While a chorus of angels did sing.

"Glory to God in the highest
Peace on earth, goodwill toward all men
Open wide your hearts to your Savior
Receive His joy, His peace deep within."

For the healing balm of His presence
Can be felt when we make room for Him
As our hearts gently cradle the Prince of Peace
Born that night in Bethlehem.

So are you willing to give Him your swaddling cloths
Surrender your all to Him
Is there a place for Him in your manger
Is there room for Him in your inn?

SOMETIMES BECAUSE OF past hurts, we put up walls. Self-protective ones erected to keep out further anguish. Unfortunately, being guarded in that way also makes it more difficult to completely experience life's joys. That being said, I have a confession to make. I really wrestled with including the following poem in the collection. Written in 1990, it is my most personal, my most revealing.

While attending a weekend retreat near Yosemite with our church's women's ministry, there was a one-hour block of time set aside where no words were to be spoken. A time we were to go off by ourselves and find a place to be alone with God. Walking the tree-lined trail, I stopped when I came to an alcove, a set of steps leading down to an area with wooden benches. Sitting down upon one of them, I quietly voiced my fears. Rejection and harsh words had so wounded and hardened my heart that I remember crying out "Oh God, I need to know. Please show me that I am loved." Looking up, I saw a twenty-foot wooden cross a few yards from where I was seated. How I didn't see it when I entered the area was beyond me. But at that moment John 3:16 was never more real to me, and I cried tears of gratitude. That very same weekend I wrote in my journal *Heart Of Stone*. Out of all of my writings, it is the only one I can quote verbatim.

"As in water face reflects face, so a man's heart reveals the man."
(Proverbs 27:19)

"I will give you a new heart and put a new spirit within you; I will take the heart of stone out of your flesh and give you a heart of flesh."
(Ezekiel 36:26)

Heart of Stone

When your spirit has been wounded
And your feelings have been bruised
Your reputation has been tarnished
And your body been abused
When you've turned inside yourself
To escape from all the pain
What can you do to end your sorrow
Feel whole and happy once again?

Heart of stone, heart of stone
Oh, my Lord, how could that be
Have I hardened my heart to others
Because of what was done to me?
Turn this stony heart of mine
Into flesh, make it new
So I can love and be loved by others
With a heart that is tender and true.

Hardened by rejection
Inside you have grown cold
Your years, they are not many
And yet you feel so very old
How you wish you could return
To when you felt so warm and free
Secure inside your mother's womb
Before one day was yet to be.

Heart of stone, heart of stone
Oh, my Lord, how could that be
Have I hardened my heart to others
Because of what was done to me?
Turn this stony heart of mine
Into flesh, make it new
So I can love and be loved by others
With a heart that is tender and true.

Drowning in tears of desperation
You have shed upon your bed
Unable to look beyond the darkness
See the hope that lies ahead
You are willing to be yielded
Yet unable to let go
Clinging tightly to your hurt
Because the pain is all you know.

Heart of stone, heart of stone
Oh, my Lord, how could that be
Have I hardened my heart to others
Because of what was done to me?
Turn this stony heart of mine
Into flesh, make it new
So I can love and be loved by others
With a heart that is tender and true.

Justifying your actions
By what you say and do
Hurting and rejecting others
Before they do the same to you
You received the Lord's forgiveness
When you called upon His name
But until you receive His love and acceptance
This song remains the same.

Heart of stone, heart of stone
Oh, my Lord, how could that be
Have I hardened my heart to others
Because of what was done to me?
Turn this stony heart of mine
Into flesh, make it new
So I can love and be loved by others
With a heart that is tender and true.

Teach me to love and be loved by others
With a heart that is tender and true.

Now for obvious reasons, *Green Eggs and Ham* was one of Samantha's favorite books when she was a little girl. Years later, *Sam I Am* was the Lord's tender yet familiar response when her heart had a love question or two about relationships.

"And do not be conformed to this world, but be transformed by the renewing of your mind, that you may prove what is that good and acceptable and perfect will of God."
(Romans 12:2)

"Love suffers long and is kind; love does not envy; love does not parade itself, is not puffed up; does not behave rudely, does not seek its own, is not provoked, thinks no evil; does not rejoice in iniquity, but rejoices in the truth; bears all things, believes all things, hopes all things, endures all things. Love never fails."
(1 Corinthians 13:4-8)

SAM I AM

I Am Sam
Sam I Am
And if you want
To be my man
Then you should know
A thing or two
Of what I will
And will not do.

I will not, will not
Compromise
Stand for lies
Or straying eyes.
I will not follow
Where you lead
For God has other
Plans For me.

Side by side
And hand in hand
Will you walk
With Sam I Am?
For I will help you
Reach your dreams
If you'll do
The same for me.

And I will be
A faithful friend
Stick with you
Through thick and thin.
But I won't give
My heart to you
Not before you say
"I do".

So you must take me
As I am
For I Am Sam
Sam I Am.

IN SEARCHING FOR love, we often forsake the sage advice of trusted loved ones and friends and go our own way. And yet these paths often lead to heartbreak. Though light-hearted in rhyme, *Humpty Dumpty* was written for one whose heart was scrambled after taking a fall.

*"Where there is no counsel, the people fall; but in
the multitude of counselors there is safety."*
(Proverbs 11:24)

*"Oh, taste and see that the Lord is good; blessed
is the man who trusts in Him!"*
(Proverbs 34:8)

Humpty Dumpty

Humpty Dumpty was a good, old egg
Who was plucked from his carton onto two wobbly legs
He rolled into the city with a plan, a great gamble
To find a love egg with whom he could scramble.

There were fried, pickled, boiled, and those over easy
And then there were those who were slimy and greasy
But his eye caught a deviled, smooth and creamy like butter
So he called off his search, and did not seek another.

Yet the king and his horses were in deep pursuit
To keep Humpty from making a mistake absolute
Blinded by love, he mistook their intentions
And his carton, their kingdom, fell into dissension.

So, brick by red brick, he erected a wall
Yet the deviled was slippery and Humpty did fall
And all the king's horses and all the king's men
Scrambled to put Humpty together again.

For his heart's yolk was broken, a runny mosaic
So a recipe was found, a special egg formulaic
An inviting aroma, his small appetite whet
They stirred in a poached, making Eggs Benedict.

Toasted muffins, crisp bacon, smothered in hollandaise dressing
And sparkling mimosas were oh so refreshing
He had gone to the city looking for a love feast
And was not disappointed, no, not in the least.

So what is the moral of this quick recipe brunch
When all the eggs in your carton unite as one bunch
Into an omelet, the king's horses and men
Are really your God, loving family and friends.

Who just want to keep you from taking a fall
Shield you from unneeded hurt, pain and harm
To help, guide and give you a safe place to land
Until you are steady and can once again stand.

For God's yolk is easy, it's tasty and light
Can flavor your life with things new, fresh and bright
And unlike poor Humpty's king's horses and men
Will lovingly put you together again.

So whether whole, cracked or broken, this Chef is by far
Tops in life's kitchen, let's give him 10 stars
Seasoned with spices both sour and sweet
Grab a knife, fork, and napkin, and Bon Appétit!

OKAY, I APOLOGIZE ahead of time for this next entry. All I can say is a mother will do just about anything to pacify her child. *Puppy Love* was written when Nathan was around three or four years old and asked for prayer for our new puppy, who was not cooperating with being housetrained.

"Every good gift and every perfect is from above, and comes down from the Father of lights, with whom there is no variation or shadow of turning."
(James 1:17)

Puppy Love

Your puppy wants to go to Heaven
But he needs to be trained the proper way
So instead of using newspaper
Pick up your Bible, kneel down and pray.

"Lord Jesus, I know that every
Good and perfect gift is from you
But this doggy's dumb and driving me nuts
And I just don't know what to do.

I know that You created him
And have placed him in our care
But sometimes he makes me feel like screaming
And pulling out locks of my hair.

You say Your love is boundless
Well it must be for You to love me
And so I'm asking for but a small portion
To pour out on this busy puppy.

So that I can love and accept him
With gratitude and with joy
And can look at him through your eyes
And see he's just a wee canine boy.

Who needs someone to guide him
To train him the proper way
A Christian doggy should behave
Each and every day.

I thank You Lord for listening
And in faith I know that You
Will help me with my doggy dilemma
And guide me in what I should do."

So now that you've prayed to the Father
Put your puppy within his care
You'd better get used to your doggy
For in Heaven you just might be seeing him there!

Detours. Don't you just hate it when circumstances take you out of your comfort zone? Change comes to everyone, and usually at the most inopportune times. Some change is welcome and promising, while others can be quite daunting.

Mary and Joseph didn't plan on having to travel when she was so near her time of delivery, but Rome had other plans. Yet when they had done all they could do, God lead them to a humble setting and provided grand things for them. Likewise, we didn't plan on traveling across the world to a new base when I was eight months pregnant, but the military had other plans. And just as God provided for the Holy Family, He did for us as well. We signed a one-month lease for a furnished apartment where we celebrated Christmas, until we were able to move into our first home a few weeks later. And as God's timing would have it, Nathan was born that very night.

Where He Leads Me was written as a reminder that while we may not see what lies ahead, the Lord does. He has already gone before us. And that's enough.

*"I will instruct you and teach you in the way you should go;
I will guide you with My eye."*
(Psalm 32:8)

"A man's heart plans his way, but the Lord directs his steps."
(Proverbs 16:9)

Where He Leads Me

I'll go where my God leads me
Wherever it may be
I'll strive to do His perfect will
Though I have yet to see
Plans mapping out my destiny
The path on which I'll trod
I'll go where're He leads me
Because I know my God
And He will never leave me
To walk this walk alone
Though far from home I'll journey
Still where He is, is home
And in my heart I'll carry Him
His love will be my guide
For in the shelter of His wings
In faith will I abide

LIKE A MOTH to a flame, people gravitate towards the light. However some luminaries can lead us astray, plunging our hearts, our lives, as well as others into darkness. *Following Yonder Star* was written when I considered the Magi that followed the star to meet the newborn King. I thought of the mad monarch jealous for his own kingdom and the ensuing massacre of the innocent. And then my thoughts turned towards today and the innocent lives being sacrificed upon the altars of choice.

"Behold, children are a heritage from the Lord,
the fruit of the womb a reward."
(Psalm 127:3)

"A voice was heard in Ramah; lamentation and bitter
weeping; Rachel weeping for her children, refusing
to be comforted, because they are no more."
(Matthew 2:18)

"Then Jesus spoke to them again, saying, 'I am the light of the world. He
who follows Me shall not walk in darkness, but have the light of life.'"
(John 8:12)

FOLLOWING YONDER STAR

Like diamonds sparkling on black velvet, so were the stars in the sky that holy night. Glittery points of light twinkling in time to the heartbeat of humanity. Suddenly the heavens were ablaze with a light so intense, a group of poor shepherds had to shield their eyes from its brilliance. Amidst the celestial fireworks, a multitude of angels proclaimed a welcome message of enduring hope. While in a distant land, learned men from the East were making preparations to follow the yonder star.

In pursuit of knowledge, their ancient writings enlightened their senses to a coming king. One who would bring peace on earth, goodwill toward men. And so they began their journey. Crossing desert sands into far away kingdoms, seeking wisdom, seeking hope, seeking peace.

Their sojourn brought them before the throne of a corrupt monarch. Years of compromise had clouded his vision, and he used oppression as a means of governing his people. Laws penned in black and white were carried out in shades of gray. Fearing the toppling of his kingdom, their tale of a child born king stirred his demon fears to madness. And he conspired to destroy the One they were seeking.

Guided by the heavenly star, their journey led them to a lowly stable. Hay and refuse lined the floor of this improbable kingdom. A feeding trough held a strange feast – a newborn wrapped in swaddling cloths, while a wee lamb serenaded the little one with melodious baas. And though the surroundings seemed surreal, a royal presence emanated from the young child. All who looked upon him sensed an authority of goodness and peace. And they offered him tangible gifts of worship and praise.

Warned in a dream of the king's pretense, the visiting Magi returned home without relaying to him the child's whereabouts. Enraged, the mad ruler dispersed his armies about the kingdom. War was waged against the innocent, as the youngest of subjects paid the ultimate price for his freedom.

2,000 years later millions of innocents have been sacrificed on that same altar of choice. Pressured to embrace immorality as truth, many are torn between holding on to their convictions and yielding to blowing winds of convenience. Concession leads to compromise as man's moral compass is directed inward rather than towards heaven. Rumors of war threaten an imagined peace. All the while latter-day saints trek across shifting sands, seeking wisdom, seeking hope, seeking peace.

But, herein lies the hope. *God so loved the world that He gave His One and only Son; that whoever would believe in Him would not perish, but have eternal life.* So choose life.

Falling snow glistens like iridescent jewels on noble trees of pine. Miniature lights twinkle in time to expectant hearts beating with the joy of the season. And like the wise men of old, may we, too, choose to follow the yonder star. For where the line of right and wrong has become blurred through reasoning, His light even now pierces ambivalent hearts, waiting to guide us into all truth.

"Westward leading, still proceeding, guide us to Thy perfect light."

LIKE MOST PEOPLE, I was saddened to hear of the untimely passing of Diana, Princess of Wales. In our idol-driven culture, many look to celebrities and public officials as people to be admired, as lights of inspiration in the darkness. Shooting stars. And yet there is one true light that outshines them all, one in whom we should all endeavor to embrace. So we must not look to the stars, but to Jesus, the One true light.

"Arise, shine for your light has come, and the glory of the Lord is risen upon you. For behold, the darkness shall cover the earth and deep darkness the people, but the Lord will arise over you and His glory will be seen upon you. The Gentiles shall come to your light, and kings to the brightness of your rising."
(Isaiah 60:1-3)

Embracing the Light

A brilliant light burst forth from the heavens, piercing the darkness. Amidst millions of twinkling points of light, this magnificent star shone its wondrous beams upon a stable in Bethlehem.

Within it's walls, were a handful of animals and a young couple, held captive by the One who lay sleeping before them. Emanating from this Little One was a presence so holy, even the creatures were silent before Him. For in this humblest of settings, a Savior had been born, who is Christ the Lord.

In fields nearby, shepherds were keeping watch over their flocks. The gentle lowing of cattle and steady bleating of sheep were a welcome respite on that seemingly ordinary night. Suddenly an angel of the Lord stood before them, interrupting their vigil, causing their hearts to become anxious and afraid. With fanfare befitting royalty, he boldly proclaimed the Savior's birth. Appearing with the angel was a heavenly chorus. Their majestic voices permeated the air with psalms of praise to God, singing "Glory to God in the highest, and on earth peace, goodwill toward men!" While the glory of the Lord shone round about them.

Following the star, the shepherds left behind their flocks seeking the One of whom the angels sang. Upon entering the stable, they saw Him. Wrapped in swaddling cloths and lying in a manger. Beholding the wee newborn, they were amazed at the wonder in what they found in Him - love, acceptance and forgiveness. Their weary hearts were refreshed and they were filled with peace beyond measure. For in His presence, it seemed as if their souls were being cradled in the very arms of God. And they bowed down and worshipped Him.

Though no longer visible, that same light still shines today. It continues to bring hope even into the darkest of hearts. Yet during these times of chaos and uncertainty, many choose not to follow. Like a moth to a flame, they are drawn instead to the enlightened messages of avid stargazers. Those psychics and seers, whose predictions shimmer with only a semblance of truth.

Still others choose to follow shooting stars, those whose lights flicker briefly upon world leaders, sport figures and entertainers. An adoring public seizes every opportunity to catch a glimpse of these rising stars, even spending their hard-earned dollars on their wares. Yet as quickly as these celebrated points of light erupt, they fall, be it by sickness, scandal or an untimely demise before horrified fans. In the twinkling of an eye, their lights are forever extinguished, plunging their skies into utter darkness.

So, during this holiday season, as the glow from our Christmas trees illuminates our homes, may the light they represent penetrate the dark, hidden places of our hearts. May it dispel the hurts, the cares, the disappointments, and fill us with a hope unlike any other. For the One we celebrate still longs to bring refreshment and peace to a weary heart. He desires to be a beacon, a ray of hope, lighting the way for those stumbling through life's dark shadows. Though there are lesser lights attempting to guide us, their radiance pales in comparison to the One true light. May it shine in us.

The piercing light of Jesus now shines brightly upon the manger of your heart. Its warmth reaches down to the innermost parts of your being. Will you not embrace it?

JUST AS LIGHT dispels darkness, so music can soothe a troubled soul. While listening to a collection of various renditions of *Ave Maria*, I was inspired to write the following piece.

On a totally unrelated note, a funny sidebar about the song happened in church one evening. I moved my purse while the pastor was preaching, which somehow managed to turn my phone on. All of a sudden, Andrea Bocelli's version began playing; rather loudly I might add, in the mid-section of the sanctuary. I struggled trying to turn it off, not realizing I had inadvertently managed to click on Pandora Radio when I moved my purse. Being new to the whole iPhone experience, my efforts to turn it off through iTunes proved unsuccessful. Those next to me also tried but to no avail. Talk about the blessings and favor of the Lord, though. Without missing a beat, the pastor made mention about the heavenly music accompanying his message. Everyone laughed, a tech savvy usher took my phone, solved the musical mystery and all was well.

Anyway, like Mary, you, too, are highly favored and blessed of the Lord.

"But the Lord said to Samuel, 'Do not look at his appearance or at his physical stature, because I have refused him. For the Lord does not see as man sees, for man looks at the outward appearance, but the Lord looks at the heart'."
(1 Samuel 16:7)

"Blessed is she who believed for there will be a fulfillment of those things which were told her from the Lord."
(Luke 1:45)

"But Mary kept all these things and pondered them in her heart."
(Luke 2:19)

"Let us hold fast the confession of our hope without wavering for He who promised is faithful."
(Hebrews 10:23)

AVE MARIA

Streaks of red coral blazed across charcoal gray skies as the day retired its colors with a fiery sunset. The heavens opened wide to reveal glittering flecks of light, while lunar beams pierced the heavens, welcoming the indigo night. Helping with the preparation of her family's evening meal, Mary's thoughts turned upward, giving thanks for blessings of family, friends and the love of a good man. Betrothed to Joseph, their announcement had generated great excitement as the town readied itself for the celebration. For the hundredth time, the young woman pinched herself, in awe of Jehovah's favor upon her life.

Lying down on her feather-stuffed pallet, she was about to close her eyes and enter into a world where dreams were as sweet as a ripened pomegranate, when a blinding light envelops her room. Shielding her eyes from its radiance, she falls to her knees as a soothing, yet commanding voice beckons her not to fear. The shaft of light fades and a heavenly presence is revealed before her. Not only were her eyes wide with disbelief, but also her heart, reeling from a message too wonderful to believe. For she, an unknown maiden, had been chosen to bear the One for whom her people had been waiting. The Messiah. Marveling at the honor bestowed upon her, she gave thanks to The Almighty, for He who is mighty had done a great thing.

Like most promises, however, the road to fulfillment was paved with adversity. Uncertainty regarding the baby's conception filled her fiancé with doubt until a heavenly messenger relieved his concerns. Mandatory compliance to the Roman Census caused the young couple to travel a great distance as her delivery date drew near. Their search for lodging led them to a stable, where she gave birth before an audience of smelly barnyard animals. An unlikely setting for a holy child surely, and yet greatness was born in humility, for He came not to be served, but to serve. Still travelers paid him homage with tangible offerings of honor and praise. While the young mother pondered all she had experienced with a grateful heart.

Ave Maria. Though some denominations practically deify her, many others barely acknowledge her significance. How remarkable her spirit must have been, though, to be chosen to raise the Son of God. For to others she may have seemed ordinary, of no exception, but God saw within her a vessel of extraordinary potential. A vessel from whom would flow the salvation of the world. For she, who was with sin, gave birth to He who was without sin. It was a miracle in every sense of the word; and one that takes place in the lives of men and women every day.

For though flawed human beings, the Lord can use each of one of us to give birth to the miraculous. Miracles of love, service and compassion just to name a few. Consider these simple, yet priceless blessings that these gifts daily bring. They initiate welcome camaraderie connecting and reconnecting lives. They soften and heal emotional wounds, bringing peace in the midst of personal storms. And when poured out upon open hearts, they unlock hidden talents and help build the confidence needed to utilize God-given abilities, ideas and inventions with wisdom and understanding.

You, too, are chosen, an ordinary vessel capable of pouring out the extraordinary. Yes, others may try to place limitations upon you, but with God all things are possible. For man looks on the outward, but the Lord looks upon the heart. And He alone knows your true capabilities and is more than able to bring to fruition all that He has planted within you. Life, liberty and a joy like none other. For He who promised is faithful. So, ponder this for a moment. What hidden miracles are you ready to release upon a waiting world? For like Mary, you, too, are blessed and highly favored.

Diamond chips sparkle amidst deep sapphire skies. Symphonies of crickets play their winged instruments in a cadence of the night.

Peace enters your room like a soft whisper, its tenderness preparing your soul for rest. And while turning back the covers of your bed, a gentle light caresses your heart and you fall to your knees in reverence. Thanking God for all of your blessings.

WHILE ENJOYING THE beauty of the heavens one evening during the holidays, my thoughts returned to the skies that used to cover us when we were stationed in Guam. The stars seemed so low, we felt we could reach up and touch them. That memory made me think of those whose lives, if only for a season, had flickered in the skies of my own life. *The Silent Stars Go By* is a result of that night of wonder. It is also the explanation of this book's dedication. A special thank you to my husband, Alton, who suggested ending the piece with the Aaronic Blessing found in Numbers 6:24-26.

"As cold water to a weary soul, so is good news from a far country."
(Proverbs 25:25)

The Silent Stars Go By

S pidery tree branches poked through layers of nature's icy white blanket. Star-kissed skies shed crystal tears, as swirling winds whispered wintry greetings. Crossing congested streets, arms filled with a rainbow of packages, her eyes were drawn to the grand illumination in Town Square. Radiant beams danced like shadows upon a cluster of skaters gliding effortlessly across the ice rink below. Serenaded by a band of carolers, harried shoppers paused from their doings to harmonize with their fellow man. Passersby offered spontaneous well wishes; while on every street corner the metallic clanging of bells signaled the call to help the less fortunate. A picturesque moment framed by Heaven's frosted glory.

Gazing upon the star atop the magnificent spruce, the woman's heart was heavy as her thoughts returned to days gone by. A string of memories wove through her mind like miniature lights on a tree. Forgotten moments now fondly remembered. And to think it all began with an act of benevolence.

Walking anxiously through the halls of her workplace, she was approached by one of the volunteers informing her of the gentleman waiting in the lobby. She had been preoccupied, so focused on the task at hand that she failed to see him sitting at one of the corner tables. As she approached him, she noticed how he looked about the large room nervously, seemingly too embarrassed to even make eye contact. And her heart was filled with compassion for she realized he was here to pick up a Christmas basket. Charitable contributions distributed to families in need during the holidays. Finding the items, she moved toward him with a cardboard box jam-packed with personal toiletries, toys, small electronics, and a large plastic bag filled with clothing. A marked difference from the colorful packages she had would later carry.

He arose quickly and they exchanged brief pleasantries. Instead, however, of handing over the benevolent items, she looked him directly in the eyes and asked how he was doing. Her genuine concern and directness momentarily disarmed him, and he began to share with her his predicament.

A successful businessman, he had an advanced degree in Management. Because of this, he never thought he would ever be in the situation in which he now found himself. Rewind to the year's beginning, and just as he had done for the past 20 years, he drove into town and parked in the garage of the building in which he was employed. A security guard met him at the front door and accompanied him to his office where he was instructed to remove all of his belongings. The failing economy had precipitated change, and his organization's solution was to downsize. With three month's severance, he packed a career's worth of memories into the provided boxes. Walking back to his still-warm vehicle, his hopes and fears of working years met unexpectedly that frosty winter morning. And his heart wailed in silent desperation.

Daily he perused the classifieds and pounded the streets and Internet in search of permanent employment. Running the numbers, he calculated their retirement would not cover their family's needs for very long. And he was correct. After a few of months, their savings was completely depleted. Though grateful for the various contract jobs he had secured throughout the year, the temporary income paid their mortgage but not much else. It bothered him greatly that his wife's childcare business, initially begun as a supplement, was now heavily relied upon as the major source of income. And he felt powerless not only by his inability to provide, but also by the mountain of debt they had incurred.

Though the woman had no words of wisdom to ease his burdens, her manner was warm and engaging and so he continued with his heart's lamentation. Overwhelmed by her willingness to listen, he began to cry. Tenderly she placed a hand on his shoulder, quietly whispering a heartfelt prayer.

"Lord, give unto Him a heart of peace
And a shoulder upon his cares to release
Abundant provisions for every day
Wisdom and hope to light his way
Make known to him your loving power
In this his deep and darkest hour."

Despair turned to hope as her tender words somehow softened the blows life had thrown his way. With arms full of blessings, he returns to his car; the sun's rays covering his heart like a mantle, as his burdens are eased with the light yoke of hope. While back in Town Square, the bells ring out a carol of "peace on earth, goodwill toward men." Swaddling her in heavenly peace.

Though a few liberties have been taken, the above illustration is true. At any point in our lives, we could be one who has fallen upon hard times. And yet in this narrative, the benevolent character is in fact you. For, if you are reading this, you are one of the bright lights that have illumined my life's path throughout the years. Your words of encouragement, compassion, provision, and even your hugs, have meant more to me than you'll ever know. And I thank you.

For like stars falling silently from midnight skies, one by one the years have disappeared with the dawn of each new day. Friends I once held dear have drifted out of my life with the passing of time. Yet I can remember your acts of kindness as if they were yesterday. And how I long for it to be yesterday once more, so that years wrapped in silence can be opened like an unexpected gift.

So this holiday as our hearts are turned towards the One whose coming has brought hope and eternal life, why not take a moment to reach out to not only those in need, but also those individuals who, if only for a season, shined brightly in the skies of your own life. Give the gift of appreciation by letting them know how your life has been enriched because of their presence. For like cold water to a weary soul, so is good news from a distant land.

116

Now may the Lord bless you and keep you; the Lord make His face shine on you and be gracious to you; the Lord turn His face toward you and give you peace.

As the silent stars go by.

TODAY MANY BELIEVE the Bible to be made up of fairy tales. The one they choose to disparage the most is of the Savior born in a manger. Well, I believe in these fairy tales. *Silent Night, Lonely Night* was written after being ridiculed by one whose beliefs differed greatly from mine.

"Professing to be wise, they became fools, and changed the glory of the incorruptible God into an image made like corruptible man – birds and four-footed animals and creeping things. Therefore, God also gave them up to uncleanness, in the lusts of their hearts, to dishonor their bodies among themselves, who exchanged the truth of God for the lie, and worshipped and served the creature rather than the Creator, who is blessed forever. Amen."
(Romans 1:22-25)

Silent Night, Lonely Night

It was a silent night, a lonely night
Within the hearts of men
As they turned their faces from
The little town of Bethlehem.

Broken, hurting, weary, empty lives
In need of one to heal
Yet denying His existence
Claiming that He is not real.

In dire need of a Savior
They instead embrace a myth
Of a mortal who brings material
Rather than eternal gifts.

Oh that we all would pause and ponder
The incarnation, virgin birth
How God left His throne in Heaven
To humbly dwell as man on earth.

To save us from destructions
Our burdens, cares, our sins
By opening up our wounded hearts
His love can enter in.

But we choose instead to be our own gods
Masters of our destinies
Would that we all could see the truth
In the nativity.

Could hear the angel's alleluias
Could hear the shepherds songs of praise
The neighing of farm animals
The barnyard anthems that they raise.

Then our empty lives could be made full
Abounding with God's love
As His blessings fall upon us
From Heaven up above.

And yet the winds of change are blowing
His flickering star grows rather dim
As the season's celebrations
Are carried out excluding Him.

A winter holiday, a festival
Celebrating nature's scene
With no reference to the Creator
Who with a word made everything.

Still there is a highlight in the season
Sharing and making memories
With faithful friends, acquaintances
And with our families.

But those moments become trampled
In the hectic Yuletide rush
Of addressing cards, of parties
Shopping malls, pageants and such.

There must be more to Christmas
Oh there must be more to life
Than this frantic, frenzied pace
Bringing tension, stress and strife.

For at the end of the day's festivities
Tissue and boxes strewn about
The jingle bells are silent
Christmas lights have been turned out.

Alone and gazing out our windows
Bellies full, hearts free from cares
With eyes turned up towards Heaven
We wonder if God is really there.

Does He really care about us
About our hopes, our dreams, our needs
That seems a contradiction
To our human reasoning.

For our minds have been enlightened
Conditioned to believe
That we as man are self-sufficient
A Savior we do not need.

And while reflecting on this Christmas
And the previous ones before
We shake our hands and wonder
What all the pandemonium was for.

What is the reason that we celebrate
The purpose that we share
This time with one another
Let them know how much we care.

Could it really have begun
In the town of Bethlehem
When wise men bearing gifts
Travelled far to worship Him.

The baby wrapped in swaddling clothes
Heaven's newborn king
The one of whom the carols
At this time of year we sing.

A tiny cry pierces the darkness
From a manger filled with hay
His cry for hearts to hold Him close
Today and everyday.

So what will be our answer
Will we heed His tender cry
By embracing Him this Christmas
On this silent, holy night.

THE 23ʳᴰ PSALM was on my heart one Christmas. At the time I thought it was an odd verse to meditate upon during the holidays; but when I heeded its message and lay down beside the still waters, I found rest for my soul.

*"I will not offer burnt offerings to the Lord my
God with that which costs me nothing."*
(2 Samuel 24:24)

*"The Lord is my Shepherd; I shall not want. He makes me to lie down
in green pastures; He leads me beside the still waters. He restores my
soul. He leads me in the paths of righteousness for His name's sake."*
(Psalm 23:1-3)

Sleep in Heavenly Peace

All was not calm. All was not bright. Threatening skies were as dark and menacing as the ravenous wolves that had attacked and scattered the flock of sheep earlier in the day. The assault had left many casualties, leaving guardian shepherds weary, drained from their exhausting watch.

Younger than most of the herdsmen, the concerned lad gently nursed the wounds of an injured sheep. Born without spot or blemish, it had been designated as the family's Passover lamb. Special care had been given to the chosen one with its soft, ivory wool. It would be the perfect sacrifice.

The lamb, however, was headstrong and stubborn. Three times the young guardian left the others in search of the adventurous stray. Three times he found it grazing near a dangerous precipice. This last time, however, he solemnly took his rod to the animal, gently breaking one of its legs. This was done to prevent the lamb from further wanderings. Once healed, the sheep would stay close to its master. Unfortunately, this also made it an easy prey for predators, and both he and his prized possession fell victim to a roving wolf pack. Blemished, there would be no lamb sacrifice. And he lifted his voice towards Heaven.

"Keeper of my heart
How I long for pastures green
Beside the quiet waters
My heart can find Your peace
Guide me with Your presence
Comfort me with Your rod
Where You lead me I will follow
You are my Shepherd God."

His lamentation was cut short when suddenly the heavens were ablaze with a blinding light. Shielding his eyes from its brilliance, an angelic being emerged proclaiming tidings of hope for all people. Joined by a multitude of the heavenly hosts, the skies were filled with joyous praise. *"Glory to God in the highest, and on earth peace, goodwill toward men!"* While twinkling luminaries accompanied the heavenly chorus.

An iridescent star shimmered like sparkling jewels upon a stable on the outskirts of town. Inside as was promised the shepherds found a baby, wrapped in swaddling clothes, and lying in a manger. His young parents slept peacefully on a mound of fresh hay, while a scattering of smelly barn animals rested quietly among them. In this humblest of settings, a sense of holiness filled the air, and they fell to their knees in worship.

It was uncanny really, for the troubles of the day seemed to disappear in the presence of the sleeping babe. The young shepherd marveled as his wounds, as well as those of his animal, were miraculously healed. With tears of gratitude flowing down his face, he knew then what he must do. He would offer his lamb to the young child. Its curly fleece would keep him warm in the harsh winter months, while its spirited nature would make for an ideal playmate. And he presented his gift to the little one.

Resting his head upon a small pile of hay, he welcomed sleep like a long-lost friend. Behind fluttering eyelids the day's events replayed like a dream in his mind. Led to pastures of fresh, clean straw, his soul had found rest. Beside the still waters of God's presence, he found peace. Closing his eyes, the boy and his lamb slept soundly before the manger. Bathed in heavenly peace.

Like the young shepherd, have you become entangled with the

pressures of life? Are you hounded by tormenting wolves of turmoil and regret? Do you feel drained from your labors, with nothing left to give? Then why not take a holiday stroll through the green pastures of The 23rd Psalm. Find comfort in the open arms of your Good Shepherd. Lay down your cares as an offering beside the quiet streams of His presence, and find rest for your soul, for He loves you. And when the day is over, and your work is done, be at peace. For His light of hope shines down on you like glittering stars across ebony skies. It's every flicker softly echoing Heaven's lullaby. All is calm. All is bright.

As you rest in His heavenly peace.

Rest. Restoration. Reassurance. Reality. The 23rd Psalm is a visual image that has always been one that I turn to when I have need of the four *"r's"* noted above. That being said, the following was written for a friend who, caught in the brambles of separation and divorce, was in need of restoration amidst the green pastures of *The Good Shepherd.*

"The Lord is my shepherd; I shall not want. He makes me to lie down in green pastures; He leads me beside the still waters. He restores my soul; He leads me in the paths of righteousness for His name's sake. Yea, though I walk through the valley of the shadow of death, I will fear no evil; for You are with me; Your rod and Your staff, they comfort me. You prepare a table before me in the presence of my enemies; You anoint my head with oil; my cup runs over. Surely goodness and mercy shall follow me all the days of my life; and I will dwell in the house of the Lord forever."
(Psalm 23)

THE GOOD SHEPHERD

As you begin your journey
Through the valley of despair
Take heart, my lamb, my child
Rest in knowing I Am there.

And I will never leave you
I Am always by your side
Under the shadow of my wings
May you rest, may you abide.

Your afflictions they are many
Yet I will bring you out of all
I Am your God, your Shepherd
And I will not let you fall.

I know what lies before you
The suffering you will bear
So cast your every care on Me
Because for you I truly care.

When you lay down in green pastures
Upon a dry and thirsty land
Like a shepherd I will lead you
Set you on your feet to stand.

And when your soul is quieted
Your mind is stayed on Me
Beside still, living waters
You'll find everlasting peace.

For I Am your God, your Shepherd
And I will restore your soul
My rod and staff will comfort you
My rest will make you whole.

Fear not, my lamb, my precious child
Place all your trust in Me
For to follow you throughout your days
Are my goodness and mercy.

And in the end, no, the beginning
Your final dwelling place will be
In my house, with Me in Heaven
For all eternity.

Yes, I Am your God, your Shepherd
Your every need, your every care
Can be met in my green pastures
Take my hand; I'll lead you there.

GRACE. A CONCEPT many of us, have trouble grasping. Sometimes we try so hard to get others to love and accept us, that we allow ourselves to be mistreated, losing our true selves in the process. Thinking that the Lord is like us, we wrongly try to work our way into His heart. Still, there is nothing we need do in order to earn His love. He just loves us because He loves us. And if we listen carefully, we can hear Him singing a love song over us. *A Song of Grace.*

"The Lord your God in your midst; The Mighty One, will save. He will rejoice over you with gladness; He will quiet you with His love; He will rejoice over you with singing."
(Zephaniah 3:17)

"For by grace you have been saved through faith, and that not of yourselves; it is the gift of God, not of works, lest anyone should boast."
(Ephesians 2:8-9)

SONG OF GRACE

Worthy, Dear One, you are worthy
Loved, Dear One, you are loved
My heart overflows with compassion
My heart overflows with love.

Cast away the cruel words that were spoken
That poisoned your heart, made it ill
Receive my love, my total acceptance
Rest in Me, my child, and be still.

For with eyes of mercy I saw you
With arms of love I embrace
No longer forsaken, rejected
Beloved, your new name is Grace.

And Grace, Grace, you are precious
Not because of the works that you do
Grace, sweet Grace, you are precious
Precious because I love you.

Yes, my heart overflows with compassion
With a love song of grace for you
A song of unmerited favor
Highly favored and worthy are you.

In the middle of the mundane, a blessing can occur if we are careful not to rush, missing the moment. That was made real to me during a visit with my parents. Now they are what you would call "old school" and have entered the 21st Century kicking and screaming, still holding on to the old way of doing things. That being said, had modern conveniences been utilized that particular day, a heart to heart moment would never have happened. For beneath the cleansing dishwater, I was *Washed In Grace*.

"And God is able to make all grace abound toward you, that you, always having all sufficiency in all things, may have an abundance for every good work."
(2 Corinthians 9:8)

WASHED IN GRACE

Life's lessons are often learned in the strangest of environments. I learned one the other day while washing dishes in the newly remodeled kitchen of my parent's home.

A military wife, reassignments had taken my family around the globe and this was the first time I had been home in years. So excited about my visit, my mother prepared a lavish meal in my honor. Similar to the one the father in the Bible prepared for his prodigal son. The inviting aroma of fresh baked bread and heavily seasoned delicacies beckoned us to linger a while at the dinner table. Conversation was peppered with laughter as memories poured freely from our hearts like sparkling water into crystal wine goblets. Afterwards, while clearing away the dishes, I started to place them in the dishwasher when I noticed that upon opening it, the original packing materials were still present. A little puzzled, I questioned my mom and was surprised to hear that she still preferred to wash all dishes, pots and pans, utensils, everything, by hand. Besides, she said it was therapeutic. I remember shaking my head in disbelief and saying something like, "Are you kidding me? You mean you have never used the dishwasher?" "That's right," she replied softly, returning her attention to storing the leftovers in the side-by-side refrigerator.

Now that explanation made absolutely no sense to me and I clenched my fists beneath the sudsy, hot water. Momentarily forgetting the feast and the hands that had prepared it, I selfishly pondered the unnecessary effort it would take to hand-wash and put away the stacks of dirty dishes piled high atop the quartz countertops. Likening the absurdity of having a sealed dishwasher to that of displaying a beautifully wrapped gift on a shelf, I inwardly reasoned that neither was worth its value until opened and used. It was at that moment, while placing a delicate porcelain butter dish into the lemon-scented water, that a still, small voice arrested my inner grumbling.

"Kind of like grace, don't you think? You see I have given my children the gift of salvation that they might live and enjoy their lives to the full, and yet some work themselves into exhaustion attempting either to please me or simply impress others. Even though it is my grace that has saved them and not their works, they continue in this way. Their services blinding them from the truth that the sacrifice I long for is a surrendered heart. Oh, if only they would take advantage of my free gift and the liberty it brings. How much more enriched their lives would be."

Those gentle words soothed the irritation I was feeling and a deeper understanding of my mom and her old-fashioned ways began welling up inside. Bowing my head before the frothy waters, I silently offered up the timeless words from David's prayer in Psalm 51: *"Have mercy on me, O God, have mercy. Purge me and I shall be clean. Wash me and I shall be whiter than snow."* Plunging rubber-gloved hands beneath the detergent waters I thanked Him for the blessing that was my mom. Tears began to flow as an unexpected intimacy arose and we began sharing things that would have remained unsaid had I just simply loaded the dishwasher. It was a holy moment.

And though after dinner clean-up that day took a little longer than usual, the simple act of washing dishes taught me a few things about my mom and myself I otherwise would not have learned. It was a moment that drew us closer together and one I will never forget. A remodeled kitchen became an impromptu classroom and a kitchen sink, the learning tool. For in surrender beauty was found in simplicity. And my soiled heart was washed in grace.

TIME STOOD STILL; or at least that's how it seemed. Wasn't it just yesterday when I followed the school bus carrying my firstborn, Veronica, off to kindergarten? Now her father and I stand watching her walk towards the large stadium with over a thousand other college freshmen for student orientation.

First Steps was written as I pondered the many steps our children take. Steps that take them away from us, and closer to our Heavenly Father's will for their lives.

"Train up a child in the way he should go, and when he is old he will not depart from it."
(Proverbs 22:6)

"All your children shall be taught by the Lord, and great shall be the peace of your children."
(Isaiah 54:13)

FIRST STEPS

I'm losing Him. I knew this day would come; yet still I am unprepared. How wonderful it has been guiding His steps this past year. Wherever He needed to go, my feet were able to take Him. Whatever He needed to do, my hands were able to assist Him. Nestled securely within my arms, together we discovered the mysteries and joys of creation. The cool waters flowing in the creek outside of town; the shade from the giant sycamore tree covering us on a hot desert day; the intoxicating fragrance of the anemones in the fields nearby. Catching raindrops with cupped hands, as well as feeling the rainwater squish between our toes; every new discovery became an adventure. All evoking shouts of glee from my Jesus as we enjoyed the beauty of our Father's world.

That all changed today. Something happened that would forever alter the way in which He sees things. Jesus walked. His first steps, though tentative at first, were replaced with more confident strides by the day's end. With each fall he took, a determined look peered back from wide, bright eyes. Though frustrated, he refused to stay down, pulling Himself up time and time again. And as His steps steadied, so did His resolve. My attempts to help him were met with resistance. I knew then that change was on the way. He would no longer be content with walking in my shoes. Directed by another, He would find His own way.

For our Father in Heaven has a plan for His life. One, I daresay, does not include my constant presence at His side. What He must do, I can be of no help to Him. Where He is going, my arms cannot protect Him. And I fear for Him.

For His heart is so tender, His spirit so gentle. Who will care for

Him, watch over Him and nurture Him as I have done? Who will cover Him with soft feathers when He is cold, give Him food when He hungers, draw water from the well when He thirsts? Who will guide His steps as He journeys the path chosen for Him? Pick Him up when He falls? Love Him when He feels lonely, unloved? Who will protect Him from the evil I sense threatening to destroy Him even now?

Yet even as I speak these words, in my heart I know. The One who will call Him will guide Him. The Lord God Almighty. He will guide Him as He guides Him even now. He will lead Him down paths of righteousness, through valleys of desolation and atop majestic mountain peaks. He will be a shield about Him, giving His angels charge over Him, keeping Him in all of His ways. He will be a light to Him that shines in the darkness, a song that arises in the wee hours. He will cause even the birds of the air to bring Him relief, drawing refreshment from wells that never run dry. For our God is the All-Sufficient One. And He alone is able to do for my son what I cannot do.

And at the end of His life's journey, The Almighty will raise Him up, bestowing upon His head a crown of glory for He will save His people from their sin. Prophecy will be fulfilled. My Jesus will reign forever, and of His kingdom there will be no end.

However, plans like this only God can bring to pass, and so I must prepare my heart for what is to come. I know not how my God will accomplish all that He has promised. But I know my God; and He is not like man that He should tell a lie. What He has said, He will do. And I trust Him.

"O Merciful Father, You have regarded this handmaiden's lowly estate, blessing not only me, but my son as well. This child, whom You have placed in my care, is such a delight. What joy He brings to my soul. For when I look upon His face, I see love there. When he throws his chubby, little arms around my neck, it is as if You, God, were holding me. And I am warmed by such great love.

Please, Lord, be merciful to me as I attempt to set His feet upon the path You have chosen for Him. Strengthen my arms as I place His life within Your hands to do with as You will. For I know that You alone are able, able to lead Him where He must go. Order His steps that He might walk in Your ways. Teach Him Your Word that He might walk in Your truth. For Your ways are right; Your word is true. Carry Him when the load He carries grows heavy; strengthen Him when His body grows weary. Please, Lord, keep His steps far from temptation. Deliver Him from those who would attempt to thwart the plans You have for His life. Protect Him, O God. Letting go of any desires I might have for Him, I yield them totally to Your will. Help me be to Him the mother He needs me to be. And when all is said and done, may our lives rise before You as a sweet fragrance of praise. For You are worthy to be praised. And I praise You."

My Jesus walked today . . . as did I. In different ways, we both took our first steps towards the fulfillment of God's will for His life. His step was physical; mine spiritual. As for now, He still needs me; and as I am able, I will be here for Him. But the time will soon come when another hand will guide Him. And on that day, I must let go. I must let Him journey the pathway paved for Him long before time began. I was told this passage would bring us great heartache, yet there is nothing I can do to prevent such pain. Being His mother, that makes me feel helpless; yet still I must trust. Trust God that my son will fulfill all righteousness. And so I will look to the One from whom my help comes. Looking in faith and with great expectation. I always knew that day would come. I just did not realize that preparing for it would begin so soon. That it would begin today. That it would begin with His first step. And it hurts.

Do you ever feel that way? With each new day, our children's steps take them down different pathways. Pathways that we ourselves may not travel - the journey to a friend's house, the time spent in a classroom, a weekend camping trip, college dorm, military assignment. No longer are they content to see the world through our knowing eyes, but feel the need to experience it through the innocence of their own. How different it is now than when we first held them. They were so fragile, so vulnerable, so dependent upon us. Yet with each step they take in life, they depend upon us less and less. Their steps take them further away from our embrace and closer to the Father's will for their lives.

And oh how it hurts.

THERE ARE TIMES when joy so fills our heart, that it spills over onto the lives of others. *And Heaven and Nature Sing* was written after wondering if the Spirit of God so filled the young child Jesus, that worship poured out from him as He enjoyed the beauty of His Father's world.

"He put a new song in my mouth, praise to our God; many will see it and fear, and will trust in the Lord."
(Psalm 40:3)

"Eye has not seen, nor ear heard, nor have entered into the heart of man the things which God has prepared for those who love Him."
(1 Corinthians 2:9)

And Heaven and Nature Sing

The Holy Child was restless. For the past two years, there had been a steady stream of visitors descending upon the tiny stable where He lived with His parents. His home was oftentimes filled with strangers and townspeople alike, who after hearing of His birth, traveled far and wide to greet Him. This day was no different. But today He was different. Today He wanted to be alone.

A nervous energy filled the young child, and was screaming for release. Rising from within the very depths of His being was a song that had to be sung. But this was not a song to be shared with shepherds watching over their flocks. Neither was it meant for the ears of weary travelers seeking the child born king. Nor was it intended for the maternal townswomen continually fussing over Him. No, this song was for His Father. His Heavenly Father. This song was for God.

Watching Him from the entrance to the stable, His mother was aware of His restlessness. Her tender heart knew her son longed to play as other children, without having crowds of onlookers observing His every move. Yet in the distance she could also see another group of sojourners heading their way. And she knew. She would have to act quickly.

"Jesus," Mary called to Him, "I saw a cluster of wildflowers near the base of that hill over there," she pointed. "I think they would be a wonderful addition for Anna's Sabbath table. Won't you go and pick a nice bouquet for me?"

The smile that lit up the toddler's face filled her with such joy that she again pondered the amazing honor that had been bestowed upon her - the honor of bearing and raising the Son of the Living

God. Oh how she loved Him, this precious gift from Heaven. Running her fingers through His wavy locks, she hurries Him along the path opposite the oncoming visitors. His pet lamb following closely at His heels.

The late afternoon sky was ablaze in color. Painted across a firmament of blue and gray were bold strokes of corals, fuchsias and violets. At the bottom of the hill was a splash of floral sunshine, framed by the descending rays of the setting sun. To the left of the knoll a babbling brook offered up watery praise. Resting upon a floating leaf was a large bullfrog, from whose expanding throat came sounds likened to the steady drumbeat of timpani. Calling birds in swaying trees lifted up their voices in harmony. Why even His little lamb joined in with a few timely "baas."

Young Jesus, arms filled with a rainbow of wildflowers, lifted His face towards the Heavens, closed His eyes and with a voice clear and strong began to sing:

> "Adonai, Adonai, how I love You
> Thank you dear God for everything
> Along with the creatures You have created
> Adonai, Adonai, hear me sing."

Unbeknownst to Him, the audience He serenaded included more than just His Heavenly Father. For when the sun began its nightly ritual, blanketing the skies in layers of ebony and gray, His parents and others had gone looking for Him. Shepherds, monarchs and townspeople alike had joined in the search. All were standing a few yards from Him. All enraptured spectators to His heartfelt praise.

In Heaven, such joy filled the Father's heart that a tear rolled down His majestic face. It could be seen on earth as a twinkling star falling from the Heavens. The throne room erupted in spontaneous praise, as a host of angels fell on their faces, giving thanks to the One who had made them.

The song reverberating through the hills that evening was a glorious one, even more wonderful than the one that heralded His birth. Witnesses to this holy moment, the small crowd was filled with awe and great wonder. Seeing the child Jesus worship so freely at such a tender age gave them pause to think on the many blessings in their own lives. Thanksgiving poured from grateful hearts. And they bowed down and worshipped Him.

While Heaven and nature sang.

This Christmas as we hustle about with our holiday traditions, may we not get so caught up in all of our busyness that we neglect to consider our own lives and the many blessings we, too, have been given - relations with family and friends, the beauty of creation, the wonder of nature. For the Creator loves us so. And as we pause from our doings, may we give thanks to the One who has given us life that we might enjoy all things. The tranquil peace of falling snow; the majestic mountain peaks poking through puffs of ivory mist; the gentle roar of the ocean as it laps quietly upon the shore. Like the tender embrace of a loved one, all are gifts to be treasured. And yet these blessings are merely the beginning. *For eye has not seen, ear has not heard, nor has entered into the heart of man the things God has prepared for those that love Him.*

Listen. Can you hear nature's love song playing softly amidst the Yuletide clatter? Do its melodies and harmonies fill your heart with awe and wonder? And is there not a song of gratitude rising up within you? If so, will you not take a moment and release it? For as you do, perhaps like the tender worship of the Holy Child long ago, the Father's heart will again be touched. A flickering luminary will traverse the midnight skies. The angels surrounding His throne will join their heavenly voices with yours.

And Heaven and nature sing.

WHILE LISTENING TO a praise song on the radio, I felt compelled to write down my thoughts. With my Bible and pen in hand, *All I Want Is You* flowed from my heart onto tear-stained pages. To this day, it remains one of my favorites.

*"As the deer pants for the water brooks, so
pants my soul for You, O God."*
(Psalm 42:1)

"My soul thirsts for God, for the living God."
(Psalm 42:2)

*"My soul longs, yes, even faints for the courts of the Lord;
my heart and my flesh cry out for the Living God."*
(Psalm 84:2)

ALL I WANT IS YOU

When I think of all the things You've done
All that You've brought me through
My heart cries out from deep within
O Lord, all I want is You.

Your love sustains me in my times of need
And guides me in what I should do
From everything within my being
O Lord, all I want is You.

Your compassions faileth not
Every morning they are new
Great is Thy faithfulness
O Lord, all I want is You.

In Your presence is fullness of joy
Sweet peace and comfort, too
To remain in Your presence always
O Lord, all I want is You.

Your word I have hidden in my heart
That I might not sin against You
And meditate on it day and night
O Lord, all I want is You.

As the deer pants after water
So my soul thirsts after You
And cries out for the Living God
O Lord, all I want is You.

Search me, O God, and know my thoughts
Try my ways and find them true
Forever will I give You praise
O Lord, all I want is You.

I'll rest in Your everlasting arms
As I give my all to You
For You are my heart's desire
O Lord, all I want is You.

I WANTED TO do something a little different when I wrote this next piece; make the message personal. So as illustrated in the story, a paper heart with the inscription: *"Peace be with you, Love Jesus,"* was included with the Christmas story in our cards that year. What touched me a few years later was when a friend opened her Bible, revealing that same paper heart. It was a tangible confirmation that sometimes it is the little things that can touch a person's heart. *And the Gift Goes On.*

"You will keep him in perfect peace, whose mind is stayed on You, because he trusts in You."
(Isaiah 26:3)

"Every good gift and every perfect gift is from above, and comes down from the Father of lights, with whom there is no variation or shadow of turning."
(James 1:17)

AND THE GIFT GOES ON

Pressed between the worn pages of her Bible was a paper heart, a gift from her beloved. Tears come to her eyes as she recycles the moment, passing it on to another.

It was Christmas Eve. Snow flurries frost the ground with layers of glistening crystal. Moonlight shimmers upon naked tree branches, while frigid winds whistle nature's evening carol. 'Tis the season to be jolly, yet there was no song in her heart, only sorrow. For she was alone, her was husband gone. Finding warmth in the arms of another.

Adding the finishing touches to her Christmas tree, she stands back to admire the work of her hands. Crowned by a vintage finial tree topper, ornaments of decoupage, encrusted jewels and reflector glass hang amidst silver and gold tinsel. A garland of fresh evergreens frames the marble fireplace, while shadows from multicolored bubble lights skip across cream-colored walls. Gracing the mantel between kindred photographs are antique figurines. Family heirlooms invoking nostalgia in both the room and her heart as well.

Yet even the familiar trimmings did little to lift her spirits, for she was tired. Tired of being alone. Tired of hurting. With the strains of *Silent Night* playing softly in the background, she is overcome by the dull, throbbing ache within her heart. And she cries.

"Oh God! All is not calm; all is not bright. Where, Lord, is this peace of which we sing? Where is your heavenly peace?"

The sudden ringing of the doorbell interrupts her thoughts. Opening the door, she looks about, but finds no one there. Thinking it to be a childish prank, she starts to close it, but stops as her eyes are drawn to an object left on the doormat. A small, brown paper package; its bow tied with seasonal raffia.

Bending over to pick it up, she noticed neither a postmark nor a return address. Inside, however, carefully wrapped in cream tissue, was a delicate paper heart. Written in red, between two stenciled Christmas hollies, were the words, *"Peace be with you. Love, Jesus."*

Seeking the bearer of good tidings, she again looks about her, only to find an imprint of footprints beginning and ending upon her snow-covered porch. And then she knew. The cry of her heart had been answered. This gift was heaven-sent.

Hand-delivered like the child born in a stable that first Christmas Eve. With no family, no friends, no midwife to assist with His birth, the young parents had to rely upon the kindness of strangers to help them in their time of need. A hastily prepared manger became His cradle. Wrapped in swaddling cloths, love shone not only from innocent eyes, but from the heavenly star spotlighting His birth. Guided by its brilliance, many traveled far and wide to greet Him.

Some visitors came empty-handed, while others brought with them small gifts for the child and His parents. In His presence, many were filled with indescribable joy, much like the one proclaimed by the angels heralding His birth; while many others were filled with a longing to repent, to change their ways. For in that lowly stable, amidst the animals, the filth, the smelly surroundings, they saw beauty. They saw the heart of God. They saw God. And they bowed down and worshipped Him.

Two thousand years later, wise men still seek Him. Yet today His light shines upon our hearts. Guiding our steps, giving us hope for tomorrow. And as He so loved then, He loves even now. Desiring to give us a rich and full life. We need only believe. Believe and receive His gift of love.

So this holiday season, instead of giving mere trinkets of affection that may tarnish, be returned or forgotten, may we purpose to present others with a gift that will last a lifetime. One that will be treasured for years to come. A gift from the heart.

Like a blazing fire, contentment burns within the young woman standing before her Christmas tree. Its fragrant aroma fills the room with the fresh scent of pine. And she sighs. Kneeling down, she returns the paper heart to its original packing, placing it amidst an array of elegantly wrapped gifts. Compared to the surrounding extravagance, it seemed plain, of little value; and yet to her it was priceless. For its very simplicity served as a reminder of the Father's love for her. For her answered prayer had fallen from Heaven like a gentle snow flurry, covering her heart with peace. And she began to sing.

"*All is calm; all is bright.*" And so it was.

Throughout the years, she has received many a gift, but none can compare to the one she received that wintry evening. For when she was without hope, it's message and the manner in which it was given her, brought hope to an anguished heart.

Seated before her now is a young man, grieving the unexpected loss of a loved one. An understanding heart hears his silent longing for relief. Removing her treasure from its place of honor, she tells him its story and tenderly places it in his hands. With the soft strains of *Silent Night* playing quietly in the background, hope fans the flickering embers of his heart. The light of heavenly peace glows through tear-filled eyes. And he finds comfort in the arms of a loving God.

As we all can. Beloved, you hold within your hands a message. Penned by the heart of God. The words are few; yet speak volumes. **"Peace be with you. Love, Jesus."**

And the gift goes on.

SOMETIMES ALL IT takes is the kindness of a stranger to stir the waters of a weary heart. The story of the lame man at the pool of Bethesda was burning on my heart the year *Touched By An Angel* was written. It reminded me that at one time or another each one of us finds ourselves before one of heaven's countless pools needing hope, needing healing, needing peace.

"What does the Lord require of you but to do justly, to love mercy and to walk humbly with Your God."
(Micah 6:8)

"Now there is in Jerusalem by the Sheep Gate a pool, which is called in Hebrew, Bethesda, having five porches. In these lay a great multitude of sick people, blind, lame, paralyzed, waiting for the moving of the water. For an angel went down at a certain time into the pool and stirred up the water; then whoever stepped in first, after the stirring of the water, was made well of whatever disease he had."
(John 5:2-4)

Touched By An Angel

A fluttering of wings, a rippling of waters, beckoned a seeking soul. Swaddling cloths covered his festering sores as he slowly made his way through Bethesda's crowded streets. Like many others, he made the yearly pilgrimage to the pool where angelic beings were said to gather. During this season of visitation, it was said an angel of the Lord would stir the tepid waters; and whoever was first to be immersed beneath its properties, was healed of whatever ailed him.

Hope burns within as he presses through the teeming masses. His steps are steady, yet his progress slow, impeded by the deformity of his limbs. Upon arriving at the pool, waters of despair douse hope's flame as he is confronted by a swarming multitude of human infirmities – the blind, the lame and the leper. Seeking a heavenly touch.

The ground trembles; still waters are disturbed as a troubled soul plunges in, finding relief, finding healing. His jubilant cries are in stark contrast to those pouring forth from one still bound in affliction. For as in years past, his trek to the healing pool has again left him unclean, unchanged. Passersby turn away in disgust, unwilling to be touched by the plight of this lowly one. Yet before him stands the One able to cleanse His wounds and make him whole. Loving hands reach out and touch one whom society deems untouchable. A feeling of peace envelops him as power surges through regenerated limbs. With great joy, he leaps as a gazelle through the maddening crowd. Giving praise to the One who has touched him.

Waves of life billow with the passing of time, while man still seeks a touch from the heavens. Swaddled in the cares of today, he inches his way through life's crowded streets in search of hope, in search of healing, in search of peace. As in times past, God still sends messengers to stir the waters of troubled hearts today. Be it by a smile, an encouraging word, a warm embrace. Yet in our strivings, we often pass them by, forgetting that by entertaining strangers, many have unknowingly entertained angels.

Like these bearers of glad tidings, we, too, can minister peace to the lost, the lonely, the hurting. We can offer hope to those whose lives have been broken, shattered by stones of abuse, rejection, disappointment. Stirring the waters of many a wounded heart, we can apply the soothing balm of God's love if we would but take the time.

However we are too busy. Our schedules are such that there is barely enough time to enjoy and attend to the needs of family and friends, much less those outside our inner circles. And though our hearts are continuously stirred during this holiday season, we offer handouts rather than helping hands; empty well wishes rather than thoughtful responses; hastily bought trinkets, rather than gifts from the heart. Our lives have become as full as the inn that turned away the Holy Family that starry night in Bethlehem. The Savior of the world had come in need of a warm bed, but instead was turned out into the cold. He had come to bring light, yet many had grown accustomed to the darkness. Would that we make room for Him in the inns of our own hearts. Would that we let His light shine in us. Would that our giving would not be as seasonal as the healings of Bethesda.

So, when the pine needles have fallen from your tree, when the priceless family heirlooms have been carefully boxed and stored away, when the light of Christmas is but a flickering shadow in your memory, may the waters of your heart again be stirred. Stirred with peace and goodwill toward your fellow man . . . the whole year through.

A fluttering of wings, a rippling of waters, beckons a seeking soul. Behold, an angel of the Lord stands before you, gently stirring the waters of your heart. Waves of life billow with a message to be poured out upon many a wounded soul. Love your neighbor. Be kind to one another. Love God as He loves you. For as you do, your life will be touched. Touched by the hand of God. Touched by His love. And perhaps, even touched by an angel.

BREAD CAN SATISFY a hungry stomach, words of life a hungry soul. *Cry Peace* was conceived and written after meditating upon the verse found in Jeremiah 6:14.

"They have healed the brokenness of My people superficially,
Saying, 'Peace, peace', but there is no peace."
(Jeremiah 6:14)

CRY PEACE

You cry peace, peace
When there is no peace
Your lives are enveloped with pain
Afflicted, tormented
Oppressed and abused
Can you ever feel whole again.

Your heartbeat grows faint
The burdens you bear
Bow you low in great despair
How My arms are wide open to hold you
Are able to shoulder
Your every care.

Still your lives are so busy
Yet empty
Days pass by as if in a blur
And you find at the end
Of another year
You are anxious and weary, unsure.

Mouthing words, singing songs
Offering rays of false hope
Attempting to win the world's favor
Of peace on earth
Goodwill to your fellow man
While your heart lies in wait for your neighbor.

Your face wears a smile
It is pasted
Hiding the tears you shed in your heart
'Tis the season for pretense
Hypocrisy
And like an actor you act, play your part.

For how can you offer another
Good tidings of joy
When the light has gone out of your life
Frustration and fear
Have brought darkness
Resentment has birthed inner strife.

Though the earth's full of My beauty
My splendor
Bound, in a rut, you cannot see
Blinded
Consumed with worry
A heart filled with anxiety.

But is there no physician
To heal you
No soothing balm to ease your pain
There is, it is I
Yet you seek Me not
Hence your suffering is all in vain.

For the hurt of My children
I ache, I grieve
My heart bleeds, the wound is severe
As I observe you forsake Me
Embracing deceit
Through self-help methods, false prophets and seers.

The earth quakes
All of Heaven trembles
As from deep within My heart does cry
Return to Me, oh wayward one
Return to Me
Lest you die.

Never to experience
The depths of my love
Never to know lasting peace
Never to completely comprehend
All your needs can be met
In Me.

For I alone know the plans
I have for you
Plans of joy, not despondency
Perfect peace can be yours
If you fix your mind
Your heart fully set upon Me.

I Am the Prince of Peace
Your Comforter
The soothing balm to ease your pain
I Am the light
That dispels the darkness
I can help you feel whole again.

Still my heart breaks as I hear you crying
Peace, peace
When there is no peace
For a world without faith
In its Maker
For a world without hope in Me.

WHAT IF A street beggar asking for help at Christmas was really an angel in disguise. *Angels Unaware* came after meditating upon that thought.

*"Are they not all ministering spirits sent forth to
minister for those who will inherit salvation?"*
(Hebrews 1:14)

*"Do not forget to entertain strangers, for by so doing
some have unwittingly entertained angels."*
(Hebrews 13:2)

Angels Unaware

She appeared to be in her mid-thirties, with a crop of matted, dark auburn hair. Her clothing hung about her in tatters; her body reeked of cheap perfume and hard liquor. Though attractive, heavy layers of makeup covered her natural beauty, while cobalt blue pierced through eyes that had seen better days. Amidst the hustle and bustle of holiday shoppers, her walk was the slow shuffle of one carrying the weight of the world upon her shoulders. Searching the masses for a compassionate heart.

Though surrounded by many, she felt alone. A throwaway from society; an outcast. Looking for acceptance, she is bumped, pushed aside and left unnoticed on the sidelines of life.

Striding confidently her way was a woman of considerable means of about the same age. Clothed in purple and fine linen, she wore about her neck a stole of faux fur. For a brief moment, their eyes met. Understanding looked back at her through carefully made-up eyes. Hope burned within the lowly one as she mustered up the courage to approach her. Yet with a flick of her professionally manicured hands, the woman brushes her aside as one would an annoying insect. The click of expensive heels resounding as a door slamming shut in her face, causing her to feel guilty for the state she is in.

For she is dirty. She is cold. She is hungry. Her steps take her past a city waste receptacle. Digging through the pile of refuse, she finds a piece of half-eaten, stale bread, which she ravishes like a starving animal. A middle-class family turns away in disgust as they witness her spiral descent through one of life's many cracks. Tears stream down her painted face, as they, too, pass her by.

Christmas carolers serenade the masses on their way to and from their yearly shopping pilgrimage. Their uplifting melodies cause many to pause from their holiday doings and listen. While the tender song of a wounded heart remains unheard among lyrical voices.

Attempting to find warmth, she covers herself with sheets of crumbled newspaper strewn about a side alley. Half-hidden in the corner is one who appears to be no better off than she was. A derelict, whose face and clothing bear the marks of one resigned to a life of mere existence. Unable to utter a sound, his hollow eyes speak volumes of compassion. Removing the frayed knit scarf from around his neck, he places his gift into small, trembling hands. Suddenly, her countenance brightens; her face beams like the radiance of a thousand suns. A feeling of peace envelops him as he turns to embrace this fellow sojourner who has likewise fallen upon hard times. Yet she is no longer there. Confused, he looks about the filthy alleyway. Even more puzzling, however, are the guttural sounds coming from his throat. Dumb since being stricken with a childhood illness, carefully sounded words now flow freely from restored vocal chords. A grace of healing pours out upon one who has shown compassion, while the contemporary strains of *Joy to the World* rise above the Yuletide clatter.

"Let every heart prepare Him room." Tears stream down his face as the One of whom they sing has come not only to the world, but into his heart as well. And heaven and nature sing.

AFTER WITHHOLDING FROM a stranger in need in order to give to my children who had plenty, conviction flowed from my heart onto paper in *The Little Drummer Boy*. Sadly, I cannot even remember the trinkets that prevented me from giving another a treasure.

"Do not withhold good from those to whom it is due, when it is in the power of your hand to do so. Do not say to your neighbor 'go and come back and tomorrow I will give it,' when you have it with you."
(Proverbs 3:27-28)

"Come, you blessed of My Father, inherit the kingdom prepared for you from the foundation of the world: for I was hungry and you gave Me food; I was thirsty and you gave Me drink; I was a stranger and you took Me in; I was naked and you clothed Me; I was sick and you visited Me; I was in prison and you came to Me. Then the righteous will answer Him, saying 'Lord, when did we see You hungry and feed You or thirsty and give You drink? When did we see You a stranger and take You in, or naked and clothe You? Or when did we see You sick, or in prison and come to You'? And the King will answer and say to them, 'Assuredly, I say to you, inasmuch as you did it to one of the least of these My brethren, you did it to Me'."
(Matthew 25:34-40)

THE LITTLE DRUMMER BOY

P a rum, Pa rum, Pa rum. The sound of small hands rapping upon twin conga drums could scarcely be heard over the din of the crowd. Weekend shoppers were hustling to and fro in this busy City by the Bay, while anxious vendors sought to relieve them of their hard-earned wages. In their harried frenzy, the crowd seemed oblivious to the desperate lives walking aimlessly about them, to the cries of the hurting, the homeless, the lost. While high above in the unseen spiritual realm, vile spirits of deception, materialism and apathy hovered about, blinding their eyes to everything, save their insatiable lusts for self-gratification and material possessions.

Pa rum, Pa rum, Pa rum. Jostling my way through the crowd, I sought to find the source of the muffled sound pounding amidst the clamor. As I neared it, I came upon a small boy, no more than ten years old, awkwardly sitting on a wooden stool near the wharf's landing. Clusters of independent seafood merchants lined the busy pier; while the smell of raw fish permeated the crisp, cool air. Seagulls flew high overhead, recklessly dropping their wares upon unsuspecting shoppers, their deposits landing only inches away from his feet. His clothing was dirty, tattered and worn; mismatched patches were sewn on short, dingy blue jeans. The soiled, tight-fitting tee shirt was inappropriate attire for the brisk, autumn winds that were whipping mercilessly about his small frame. His intermittent shivers out of sync with his drumbeats.

Pa rum, Pa rum, Pa rum. Still he plays on. The beating of the drums sound out the monotonous rhythm his life has become. Passersby walk around him as if he were not there. Only the sporadic clinking of coins in the rusty tin broke the rhythm of his drum song.

I wonder if those coins would later buy his family's evening meal. For shame and embarrassment peek through the hollow eyes of a child forced to grow up too quickly. Left alone to fend for himself, he marches to the tune of a different drummer.

Pa rum, Pa rum, Pa rum. Yet still he plays on. And as I stand there watching him, compassion wells up within me. My mother's heart is stirred as I long to wipe away the dirt and grime from his wind-blown cheeks, and to straighten the small, knit cap that fails to cover his ears.

And as I gaze upon this unlovely one, my thoughts turn to my own dear children, whose days are spent laughing and playing, discovering the many blessings life has to offer. They neither worry nor fret about their needs being met; and yet there he sits, brow furrowed, his shoulders stooped from the heavy load he was not meant to carry. Though he appears to be about the same age as my eldest child, their lives are as light-years apart. The realization of that truth fills me with compassion, and I wonder why they, and not he, are the fortunate ones in this never-ending song called life. He did not choose, neither was he responsible for the state his life is in, and yet responsibility appears to be his just the same. And while I feel sorry for him, at the same time I feel guilty. For though we are by no means wealthy, our lives have been made rich by the special love we share with one another, a love that seems sadly alien to him.

Pa rum, Pa rum, Pa rum. And still he plays on. Rummaging through my purse, I search for an offering to present to the young musician. I find, however, only enough money set aside for the little mementos I had intended to buy for my own children. How can I take from them and give to one who is not my own? On the other hand, how can I deny one who is in dire need by giving in to the mere wishes of others?

And as I stand there pondering what to do, the pleading eyes of that little boy stare at me, tugging at my heartstrings. I struggle with the conflicting thoughts and emotions warring within my being. Wanting desperately to do the right thing, I hesitate. The picture of returning home empty-handed to the disappointed faces of my children plays across the wide screen of my mind. And deep down I know I cannot disappoint them, no matter what the reason. Running my fingers through my hair in frustration, I turn and walk slowly away. Guilt and shame burn within my bosom for I realize I am far worse than those who just pass him by. For though I paused from my own hectic life to pay notice to one of society's outcasts, I am no different, for I, too, do nothing to aid him in his plight.

Pa rum, Pa rum, Pa rum. Walking away, my eyes return again to the child, who is now becoming smaller as distance grows between us. Despondency stares back at me from young, knowing eyes that have seen far too much for their years. As the gap between us fills with moving bodies, he becomes just another blurry face in the crowd. Still I walk on. A lone tear falls to the ground, only to be crushed by the parading feet of an apathetic people. While about me, the wind whistles the shrill cries of revelry, as unseen spirit beings rejoice for yet another desperate life remains trapped in hopelessness and despair. And another is now bound with condemnation and regret.

It is weeks later now, and I find myself clearing away and loading the Christmas dinner dishes into the dishwasher. After turning the start button to the on position, I join my family in the den, where they are playing games in front of a roaring fire. Their happy bantering fills the room with joy and laughter, and my heart is warmed as I join in the evening's merriment. Contentment shines bright on each face, like the fire's glowing embers. Its flickering flames bring a radiant light into our home. And I find comfort in this familial intimacy.

It is while enjoying this moment that the rattling of eating utensils against the dishwasher's inner walls brings to my mind the street performance of a little drummer boy. The sound of his playing once again beats loudly within my heart. And as I think of the shivering child, surrounded by many, yet all alone, I begin to weep. For the rhythm he beat out on his drums was a desperate plea for help; yet like many others, I was unwilling to answer his call. I was unwilling to be used as an instrument, offering hope and encouragement to him. I was unwilling to sacrifice my own desires and show him a little human kindness. I was unwilling to convey to him that his life does have worth and meaning by acknowledging him as a viable member of society. And most importantly, I was unwilling to share with him that a bright future is his to have if he would only believe and trust in the One who holds the future in

His hands. No matter how seemingly valid the reason, the truth remains the same. I was able, yet unwilling, to help.

Remorse flows through my veins as I pray now that he does not go to bed hungry. I pray that he dresses warmly and has a roof over his head. I pray he is allowed to play, as children should, without being saddled with adult responsibilities. I pray that his heart is filled with joy and his mouth overflows with laughter. And lastly, I pray that my guilt-ridden prayers will somehow be of help to him, as I can do nothing else for him now. With the flame of conviction burning within my heart, I vow never again to let an opportunity of sharing hope with one in need pass me by.

Pa rum, Pa rum, Pa rum. Somewhere in the Bay Area, a little drummer boy walks it's busy, crowded streets. The lonely rhythm of his drum song beats softly amidst the cacophony. Yet in my heart it beats louder still.

A HOMELESS MAN gave his heart to the Lord, was baptized and became a member of our church one Sunday. He died suddenly two days later. Estranged family members neither wanted to honor his life with a funeral nor a celebration service. The thought that one could live and die, and have loved ones seemingly unconcerned with his passing, caused me to write *Fly*. For no one is invisible. God sees us, every one.

"Are not two sparrows sold for a penny? Yet not one of them will fall to the ground outside your Father's care."
(Matthew 10:29)

FLY

He sees the tiny sparrow
When it falls down from the tree
Sees the wind that blows
Over earth and land and sea
Catches every falling tear
Hears the crying heart
Nothing is concealed
He even numbers all the stars

More valuable than silver
More precious than you know
Little fallen sparrow
How the Father loves you so

He sees the unlovely
The unwanted, castaway
The ones whose lives have turned
Into an endless darkened day
He feels their rejection
Their anguish, hurt, their shame
Though forgotten by so many
He knows them all by name

More valuable than silver
More precious than you know
Little fallen sparrow
How the Father loves you so

And into arms of mercy
He gathers every one
Little fallen sparrow
Welcome home

More valuable than silver
More precious than you know
Little fallen sparrow
How the Father loves you so

Little fallen sparrow
Heaven hears you cry
Into the arms of your Creator
Fly

WHILE RIDING IN the backseat of a taxi in Midtown Manhattan, my eyes were drawn to the carriage horses lining the streets near Central Park. The thought came to me that like those animals, many of us find ourselves in oppressed situations; circumstances that cause us to become shackled by the cares of life. It is during those times that we must remind ourselves that there is a God who sees us. And He loves us. A special thank you to my son, Nathan, who helped me harness and convey the emotions I was feeling while writing *Carol of the Bells*.

"He heals the brokenhearted and binds up their wounds."
(Psalm 147:3)

*"The thief does not come except to steal, and to kill,
and to destroy. I have come that they may have life,
and that they may have it more abundantly."*
(John 10:10)

*"These things I have spoken to you, that in me you may
have peace. In the world you will have tribulation; but
be of good cheer, I have overcome the world."*
(John 16:33)

CAROL OF THE BELLS

Rustling winds fingered nature's invisible keys, scattering falling notes from overcast skies. Musical artists serenaded shoppers and passersby with holiday carols. A garland of bells jingled in perfect harmony, and yet the creature was out of sync with the perpetual rhythm of life.

For staccato movements hindered its natural flow. Instead of moving freely, the animal was part of a winding line of carriage horses used for recreational travel. An irony considering it was predisposed for solitary transit. With a tour guide at the reins, it escorts paying customers down landmark streets and tree-laden parks. Innate desires to roam and explore are stifled. Like wooden horses on a carousel, it goes up and down a preset route to pre-recorded music.

Inhumane conditions turn this magnificent creature into a beast of burden. Emaciated, its muscles are now atrophied. Movements to exhibit strength are discouraged by the use of horsewhips. Tightly secured mouth bits reinforce compliance. It struggles putting one foot in front of the other. While the adornment of feathers and beads mock its repression.

For like wallflowers, the horse line languishes silently on city curbsides. The dull sound of worn shoes replaces thundering hooves. Beaten down and shackled, they are unaware one swift kick of a shriveled limb could render their captors powerless. And so they remain broken; heads bowed low, their wills tethered to an invisible harness. The occasional stamping of a front leg is their only outward sign of protest. While descending raindrops frame their shame between clouded skies and concrete pastures.

Does the above illustration strike a dissonant chord upon your heartstrings? Do you feel invisible, trapped in a life in which you merely exist? Is your past robbing you of your present, while casting shadows on your future? If so, you may be like those pulling their weighty wagon of woes behind them while the band plays on. Caught in the brambles of circumstances, wrong choices or even the actions of others, they feel powerless, choosing instead to cower in defeat. Disgrace covers them like a shroud. Their lives have become a merry go round of lost hopes and broken dreams. They travel in circles, seeking the brass ring of relief. Grasping vainly after the wind.

For they have forgotten they were created in the image of Almighty God. Created to live a full and abundant life. However, many settle instead for much less. But His plans are for good and not evil, to give a future and a hope. And there is no hope in oppression. Neither is there a place of honor for ribbons of regret to hang from your heart's shelf. No, you were made for so much more, Dear One. For clothed in Christ Jesus, you are a trophy of His goodness, a garland of His grace. Surrounded by His truth you were meant to walk in confidence; knowing that the One who created you is able to keep you. Yes in this world there will be difficulties, but take heart. Our God has overcome every trouble under the sun. And He is more than able to handle yours as well.

So let go of what has been holding you back and allow the Lord to roll away the clouds, letting His light shine upon your path. Step out from among the shadows, finding rest in His green pastures. Give all your concerns to Him for He cares for you. And fear not, for God is with you. Longing to quiet you with His peace, while removing the heavy yoke from upon your shoulders. For He came that you might be free. Free to enjoy the life you have been given. Listen. Can you hear His bells of freedom ringing? They ring for you. Oh, how He loves you.

Thunder rolls across weeping skies releasing brilliant flashes of light. Skillful musicians accompany a trio of singers crooning seasonal favorites. All the while a lowly creature shuffles along the concrete pasture. Its carol of bells a syncopated rhythm in the music of life.

Ding-dong; ding-dong.

FREEDOM IS NOT free. No one knows that better than our Heavenly Father. For out of a great love for us, He sent His only Son, Jesus, to pay the ultimate price for our debts, that we might be free.

This next entry is an odd one to be included in a holiday devotional, but I do so anyway with great pride. My dad and husband were both career Air Force, and it seems my son may be following in their footsteps. *Freedom Is Not Free* is dedicated to the men and women in the Armed Forces who serve both at home and abroad, in wartime and in peace. Whose dedication to service separates them from loved ones during birthdays, celebrations and holidays. And to their families keeping the home fires burning until their return.

"For you, brethren, have been called to liberty; only do not use liberty as an opportunity for the flesh, but through love serve one another."
(Galatians 5:13)

FREEDOM IS NOT FREE

Why do we call it freedom
When freedom is not free
The cost was blood and sweat and tears
That bought our liberty.

Look beyond our nation's banner
Waving proudly in the breeze
Across the plains and mountains
Thru the valleys, o'er the trees.

And see a people of variety
Living side by side
In God we trust, our motto
Just laws our leaders' guide.

Yet some still take for granted
They neglect to understand
How great a sacrifice was made
To dwell in this free land.

For many left behind their loved ones
Their friends, their families
Standing true to oaths once taken
To defend our liberties.

Holding fast they fought for freedom
Both at home and then abroad
Spilling blood upon the waters
O'er the grounds on which they trod.

Wounded from the many battles
In mire and blood their bodies lay
The dead with mouths wide open
Forming words they'll never say.

Seeing eyes no longer seeing
Hearing ears no longer hear
Hearts once beating stilled and quiet
Loved ones close no longer near.

And though their hopes and dreams were shattered
Let their deaths not be in vain
We must keep forever burning
Freedom's torch, the victor's flame.

For they died for you, America
Your freedom was not free
For 'twas their blood and sweat and tears
That bought your liberty.

So when you speak again of freedom
May your hearts be filled with pride
And gratitude for those
Who for your freedom fought and died.

"Peace on earth, goodwill toward men." A phrase that triggers not only cherished memories of Christmas, but also vague moments of holiday helter-skelter. In retrospect, I realize that so much time was spent trying to perfect and create special moments, that I missed them entirely. *Repeat the Sounding Joy* became a personal call to savor the moment; a call to look at each new day as a child looks forward to Christmas – with great expectation of the gifts we are about to unwrap.

You will show me the path of life; in Your presence is fullness of joy; at Your right hand are pleasures evermore."
(Psalm 16:11)

REPEAT THE SOUNDING JOY

Cerulean skies shimmer beneath the moon's silvery light. Celestial luminaries twinkle silent accolades, while wintry winds herald nature's frosty tidings. Like glittering fireworks, bursts of joy explode in holiday hearts while the songs of the season resound across the airwaves. Christmas. The time when dreamers dream and wishers wish upon a midnight clear.

And yet tranquil skies are a stark contradiction to the gale winds blowing throughout the lives of people today. Whirling layers of darkness uproot foundations, scattering property and lives in its wake. A failed economy yields rising debt and unemployment. Anger fuels unspeakable acts of violence, victimizing the unsuspecting and the innocent. Hearts fail daily from the unrelenting pressure placed upon them. And like the shepherds keeping watch over their flocks that night, they are in need of a heavenly presence proclaiming tidings of comfort and joy.

Ever wonder what it would it be like today if we could see and hear the skies ablaze with the glory of God's presence? Scripture says that in His presence is fullness of joy; strength for today and hope for tomorrow. Can you imagine how it would feel to be invigorated as the weight of your burdens and cares simply vanish amidst the blinding light of His grand celestial display?

We need only look at a young child during the holidays to get a glimpse of how this might feel. No matter what disappointments or hurts he may have experienced, they fade with the dawn of the first Christmas light. Like electricity, the air is charged with excitement, adrenaline speeds expectant hearts, as packages are hastily unwrapped; the hidden contents revealed and appreciated beneath twinkling miniature lights. And like dominoes, joy falls onto others with infectious delight.

Somewhere along the way, however, many lose that child-like enthusiasm. Their joy evaporating like vapor rising from a steaming cup of coffee. This author, I must confess, can attest to that fact. Once a dreamer, I dreamed dreams yet to be realized. When I was a child, I envisioned life filled with adventure and happily ever after. My Barbie dollhouse set the stage for many unscripted plays on the idyllic life. With my imagination actively engaged, excitement grew as adolescent expectations of love and happiness became embedded deep within my heart. Disappointments were cast aside as one casts a fishing line into watery depths. And I went out each day, fishing for joy.

But as I grew older, discontent and regret began to weigh heavily upon me and my heart sank, submerged beneath murky waters of melancholy. For in striving for perfection, I missed so many moments, so many opportunities to enjoy the life I'd been given. My attempts to make certain everything was done decently and in order frustrated myself and loved ones as well. Because running a tight ship keeps everyone just a little on edge. Guess I must have missed the memo that doing things the right way could also be enjoyable. Please join me as I highlight a few of those holiday misses.

With a desire to honor the Reason for the Season, my perfectionism naturally intensified during the Yuletide. Checklists were made, revised and amended. Seasonal carols played continuously in the background, boxed cards were carefully selected to go along with that year's Christmas writing, while all decorative elements were color-coordinated and themed, each one meticulously placed and hung throughout the house in precisely the same manner every year. Even the toilet roll angel, lovingly handcrafted by one of the kids, had its special place on the tree. But I digress.

Anyway, with the exception of our middle child, who would either be sewing ribbons on her pointe shoes or busy with Nutcracker rehearsals, the rest of the family would be in the den sipping marshmallow-covered hot chocolate, while watching a myriad of holiday specials. All keeping out of the way of the crazy woman running around like a headless chicken, adding finishing touches to the holiday decor. We were going to have a Merry Christmas, by golly, and it was going to look like Better Homes and Gardens in the process. If only I had learned to whistle while I worked. What songs of bliss may have been composed in the process. For joy can be found in the journey.

Those innate tendencies trickled down to all areas, even gift presentation. Case in point, our eldest, loved creating and putting things together. Why until she went away to college, she pondered becoming an architect, building miniature Lego houses, as well as drawing and designing various floor plans throughout her middle and high school years. Anyway, when she was around seven years old we purchased a Victorian dollhouse for her. It was an elaborate two-story structure, complete with three floors of rooms, two staircases, flower boxes and hundreds of pieces. At my insistence, her dad assembled what I knew would bring her countless hours of imaginary pleasure. It took him from midnight until 6AM Christmas morning to do so. After all, visions of her excitement danced through my head as she saw the assembled gift in all its glory, culminating with her subsequent foray into imaginary playtime. But, alas, that's not exactly what happened. She squealed with delight of course, and then to her dad's horror, immediately disassembled the entire dollhouse. Every piece. Her reassembly took less than one hour. The look my husband gave me that year let's just say is forever etched in my memory.

Moving on. Sometimes my attention to minor details caused me to miss the obvious. Like the time I went to great lengths decorating the large Spruce we had secured at a local Christmas tree lot. Adorned with magnolias, pinecones, eucalyptus, red berries, baby's breath and yards of gold ribbon laced throughout, it took days to decorate and get it just right. It was a beautiful accessory for the squadron party we hosted that year.

Now out of all of the kids, our youngest, who was four years-old at the time, was truly enamored with and used to spend hours looking at the tree, mesmerized by the blinking lights and the various ornaments. However, after a couple of weeks, I noticed an unusual sprinkling of evergreen needles on the carpet, and began vacuuming and filling the tree stand with water almost daily. Then the branches began to turn brown. It was then I noticed that the carpet surrounding it was completely saturated. It seems there was a leak in the tree stand. And so three days before Christmas, I took down the dying Spruce and placed it on the curb outside of our home. (Cue musical finale from Tchaikovsky's *Swan Lake*.) When our preschooler came home from school that afternoon and saw his precious tree discarded on the curb, what he did next just about broke my heart. That little guy ran over to the tree, dragged it from the curbside, down our sidewalk and was attempting to lug it up the front steps back into the house. With tears streaming down his face, he repeatedly cried, "No! Don't take my Christmas tree! Don't take my Christmas tree!" Picking him up, I kissed away his tears and carried him, broken heart and all, back into the house. A small decorative plant from our den became our *Charlie Brown Christmas* tree that year. A moment in time that could have been easily averted had my attention to minutiae been focused on the fundamentals of tree maintenance rather than aesthetics.

And finally, there was the time when I tried to impress by creating, rather than enjoying the moment. My parents had just flown in from out of town and it was their first visit to our new home in Virginia. While they were retrieving their suitcases from the minivan, I wanted to create a welcome holiday atmosphere and went inside, turned on all of the Christmas lights, popped in a Christmas cd, and lit the fireplace.

What I failed to do in my attempt to impress, however, was open the fireplace flue. Within minutes, smoke began filling the room, setting off the security alarm, which at 10PM that night kept resounding, "Warning! You have violated a secure area! The police have been called! You must evacuate the area!" Like a scene out of a slapstick comedy, we ran around opening all the windows and doors in the great room attempting to clear the air, but to no avail. My dad rushed back into the garage, brought out, plugged in and starting using the electric leaf blower to rid the house of the thick smoke. His valiant efforts, however, rearranged furniture, displaced a few pictures off the walls and incited the family pooch to howl along in protest. When the policeman arrived, the smoke had cleared a little, though the alarm and canine were still vocalizing caution in two-part harmony. He took in the scene, blower and all, and tried to remain professional, but a small smile could be seen curling at the sides of his mouth. My husband looked at me, shook his head and with a sheepish grin said to my parents, "Welcome to our home." To this day when I go to light a fire in the fireplace, he asks if the flue is open.

Memories – those precious moments drawn from the wellsprings of our minds. Moments sprinkled with golden days, gloomy forecasts and good intentions gone awry. So when thunder and lightning rage across the skies of your lives, draw deep, remembering the blessings you have been given. Remember also that the One who placed the stars in the skies, also holds your very breath in His hand. In the midst of trouble, sense His comforting presence near you. Be amazed, as your cares seem to fade under the light of His infinite love. And don't miss those spontaneous moments by striving for perfection. Enjoy the journey. Embracing each day as if it were Christmas. For happiness is based upon circumstances, but true joy can be found in focusing on the presence and goodness of God. For the Creator of the Universe awakens you each morning with the gift of a new day. So open it with expectation as He breathes life into His plans for you. For He loves you more than you can even imagine. This writer vows to do the same.

And so I thank you for accompanying me down memory lane. Doing so has reminded me of yesteryear's experiences and I am truly grateful. For I have been blessed with loving relationships, good health and a reasonably sound mind – the latter point my family would probably beg to differ. But again, I digress. I simply ask for one more indulgence as I feel the need to have a Charles Dickens moment. (Cue a pensive *Prelude and Fugue* from Johann Sebastian Bach.) "Holy Spirit, I will honor Christmas in my heart and try to keep it all the year, enjoying life and every moment I am given."

And now fellow traveler, I wish you a life filled with God's unlimited favor and goodness. May your heart be light as you enjoy your life's travels, dreaming dreams and wishing for things yet to be. And like a rainbow after a rain, may you be covered with colors of peace. For 'tis the season to be jolly; so cast out a line of hope and fish for joy.

Crystal stars shimmer like specks of glitter against indigo skies. Yuletide carols fill the air with familiar melodies, stirring expectant hearts to sing. Living happily in the moment, new memories are made as merry sounds of joy resound and are repeated. You know, my parents will be with us again this Christmas. Better keep that leaf blower handy.

REMEMBER THAT *I Love Lucy* episode where Lucy meets a group of outcasts called The Friends of the Friendless? A ragtag band of misfits who felt forgotten by society? Well, though we may forget God, He will never forget us. In fact, our names are engraved upon the palms of His hands. A truer friend we will never find. So let's drink a cup of kindness yet for *Auld Lang Syne*.

"A man who has friends must himself be friendly, but there is a friend who sticks closer than a brother."
(Proverbs 18:24)

"Turn us back to You, O Lord, and we will be restored; renew our days as of old."
(Lamentations 5:21)

AULD LANG SYNE

Happy New Year! With a glass of sparkling wine and a piece of sourdough bread, she ended the year the same way she began. Having communion with an old acquaintance. Actually, he was more than an acquaintance; he was her closest friend. One that Anne of Green Gables would say was her bosom friend. And faithful. He had been there for all of her firsts. First breath, first word, first step, first heartbreak. From kindergarten to college, to the long walk down the aisle where she married the man of her dreams, he was there as the unseen guest in the celebration known as her life. His very presence brought a comforting sense of peace. And it felt like home.

It hadn't always been that way, though. There was a season in her life when she considered him to be nothing more than just a childhood memory; a friend that she had seemingly outgrown. Seeking her own way caused her to neglect their friendship. And yet those years, though adventurous, were also her loneliest. For though it may have been a time of personal and professional growth, it always felt like something wasn't quite right. Something seemed to be missing. And she couldn't put her finger on who or what that might be. All the while the face of her friend rarely crossed her mind, though she was never far from his.

But, that all changed last New Year's Eve. Like a dancer, the flames from her fireplace moved rhythmically to the sounds coming from the flat screen TV mounted above the mantle. With a glass of sparkling bubbly in her hand, she welcomed the year's first moments watching hundreds of thousands of strangers celebrating the ceremonial ball drop in Times Square. As the fireworks outside her house sprinkled the skies like a cluster of shooting stars, an overwhelming sense of nostalgia fell upon her. She thought of loved ones and friends with whom many a precious moment had been shared. Of her adult children celebrating with their young families out of state. And finally her mind lingered upon the tender kisses she and her late husband would exchange at the midnight hour. Oh, how she missed them. Her gratitude for their presence in her life filled her with longings for yesteryear, and she began to cry. Cry out to the one she left behind.

And as the last firework sizzled, its tail trailing like sparks of fiery confetti, she found her friend where she had left him – in her heart. The familiar sense of comfort enveloped her being as she became reacquainted with His presence. He neither mentioned nor condemned her years of silence, but welcomed her back with open arms. Everything old became new again as she found comfort and joy in His presence. Slicing a piece of bread from the fresh loaf on the counter, she poured a glass of sparkling wine and shared the first meal of the year with her beloved friend. God.

How does the first line of that classic song go? *"Should old acquaintance be forgot and never brought to mind . . ."* And yet, how many times do we go through our days without even acknowledging our eternal friend, the Ancient of Days? Creator of time and eternity, He knows us better than we know ourselves. For He alone is acquainted with all of our joys and sorrows. He knows all we have and ever will experience. Why even the hairs on our head He can number. And yet He is often placed upon the backburner of our lives, the memory of him growing fainter with each passing day. As we douse the embers of camaraderie with waters of neglect.

So at this time of the year when our minds take sentimental journeys through golden days of yore, how much more should we reacquaint ourselves with the One who breathed His very life into us. The One who accepts and loves us unconditionally. For one thing remains constant and will never change. He is the friend who sticks closer than a brother; who promises to never leave nor forsake us; who is never too busy to answer when we call. We may become distracted and lose our way, but like a good shepherd, He will find us. Leading us safely back to where we can once again graze upon His goodness and mercy in a place called home.

And so, why not ring in the New Year by breaking bread with Him; partaking of the new life that is to come. And take your cup and drink to all that He has done. For God so loved that He gave. Gave His only Son, not to condemn, but to save. Save all who would believe in Him. And there is no greater love than this, than to lay down one's life for a friend. Oh how great a friend is He.

Swarovski crystals sparkle like diamonds as the illuminated orb welcomes the New Year in a spectacular fireworks display. Breathing in the hope of a new year, the woman's passion for life is reignited. For what is, is now past; and what was to come, is now present. The future is but a blank slate ready to be inscribed. And she sighs. Sharing the moment with her eternal companion.

We can do the same. *So let's drink a cup of kindness yet for Auld Lang Syne.*

EPILOGUE.   I FELT it was only fitting to end this collection with a message that is from God's heart, to mine, to yours.   Hold on to your dreams.   For in them lies a hope.

"For lo, the winter is past, the rain is over and gone. The flowers appear on the earth; the time of singing has come."
(Song of Solomon 2:11-12)

"For I know the plans I have for you," declares the LORD, "plans to prosper you and not to harm you, plans to give you hope and a future."
(Jeremiah 29:11)

"Let us hold fast the confession of our hope without wavering, for He who promised is faithful."
(Hebrews 10:23)

DREAMGIVER

A dream was birthed within Me before time began. It was a wonderful dream, bursting with hope, filled with promise. I saw you standing in it, tall and confident; fulfilling the purpose my Father has for you. You did not worry about what others thought. Your only concern was to do His will, no matter the cost. And it did cost you. Friends and loved ones you held dear discouraged and mocked you. They shot you down time and time again with doubting darts of scorn, of unbelief. And as your wounded heart lay bleeding upon life's battlefield, insecurities hovering over you, you closed your eyes and listened for that still, small voice inside. And oh the peace that came over you. For you knew that it was my Father who began and was working this dream in you. Not for your purpose, nor your pleasure, but for His. And so you pressed on.

At times you felt alone, but you were not. I, too, was in the dream. I walked alongside you down the road of lost hopes and broken dreams, retrieving your hopes, rebuilding your dreams. I held you when you grew weary, your soul downcast in the Valley of Despair. I gave you refreshment from my rivers of living water as you wandered in the dry, barren, seemingly endless Desert of Preparation. My hands, my heart, my mouth joined yours in lifting up praises to my Father atop the High Places – the mountain wherein dreams, given in the stillness of one's heart, come true.

And they do come true. So do not let go of your dreams, Dear One, for in them lies a hope. Hold fast to them for I breathed their very life into you. And do not consider it strange the conflicting emotions that will assail you, for I felt them, too. I, a fellow traveler, who journeyed down a similar road, driven by a promise that burned within Me. How full of hope I was that my dream would be realized. Yet, like you, I met resistance every step of the way. I could have given up, but I knew my Father and His nature. I knew that He was faithful to carry me to the fulfillment of my dreams, to the mountaintop. And so I pressed on. Mocked, scorned, beaten, I was lifted high in shame for all to see; yet my eyes remained fixed upon the One who sent Me. The One who now sends you.

So, again I say, do not let go of the dream planted within you. For as did mine, yours, too, will bud, flowering triumphantly into reality. Though it does not appear to be so now, be encouraged, for it will grow, flourishing as a well-watered garden. Its beauty will be a sweet fragrance that will envelop not only you, but also those who dare to gaze upon its loveliness. *For you see, the winter is past, the rains are over and gone; the flowers appear on the earth, the season of singing has come.*

Like a child inside its mother's womb, a dream grows in the stillness of your heart. And on this your journey to its fulfillment, set not your eyes, your hopes, upon your dream, but look instead to Me. Trust in Me and in my ability to do as I have promised. Believe in your heart that I am with you and that I love you. For I am, and will remain as always, Jesus, your *Dreamgiver.*

Thank you so much for taking this journey with me through the pages of *Tidings of Comfort and Joy*. I hope that you will carry within your heart a precious memory or two. Should a recollection linger, please share your experience on fromcherylsheart.com. I'd love to hear from you.

Now may the light of His love shadow you, the wind of His presence refresh you and His river of peace surround you, as you go out, living each day with great expectation - fishing for joy.

~ Cheryl Berger

ABOUT THE ARTIST

Stacy Jordon and the author met through a mutual friend at a ladies Bible study. She has two passions in life – God and Art. There is nothing that makes her soul sing louder than putting the two together and sharing them with others. She loves teaching His Word and creating paintings that reflect His Word. Stacy and her husband, Billy, live in Atlanta with their two sons and a very photogenic cat, whose image often graces the canvas of many of her pieces. Information on the artist can be found at stacyjordon.com.

Made in the USA
Columbia, SC
15 July 2017